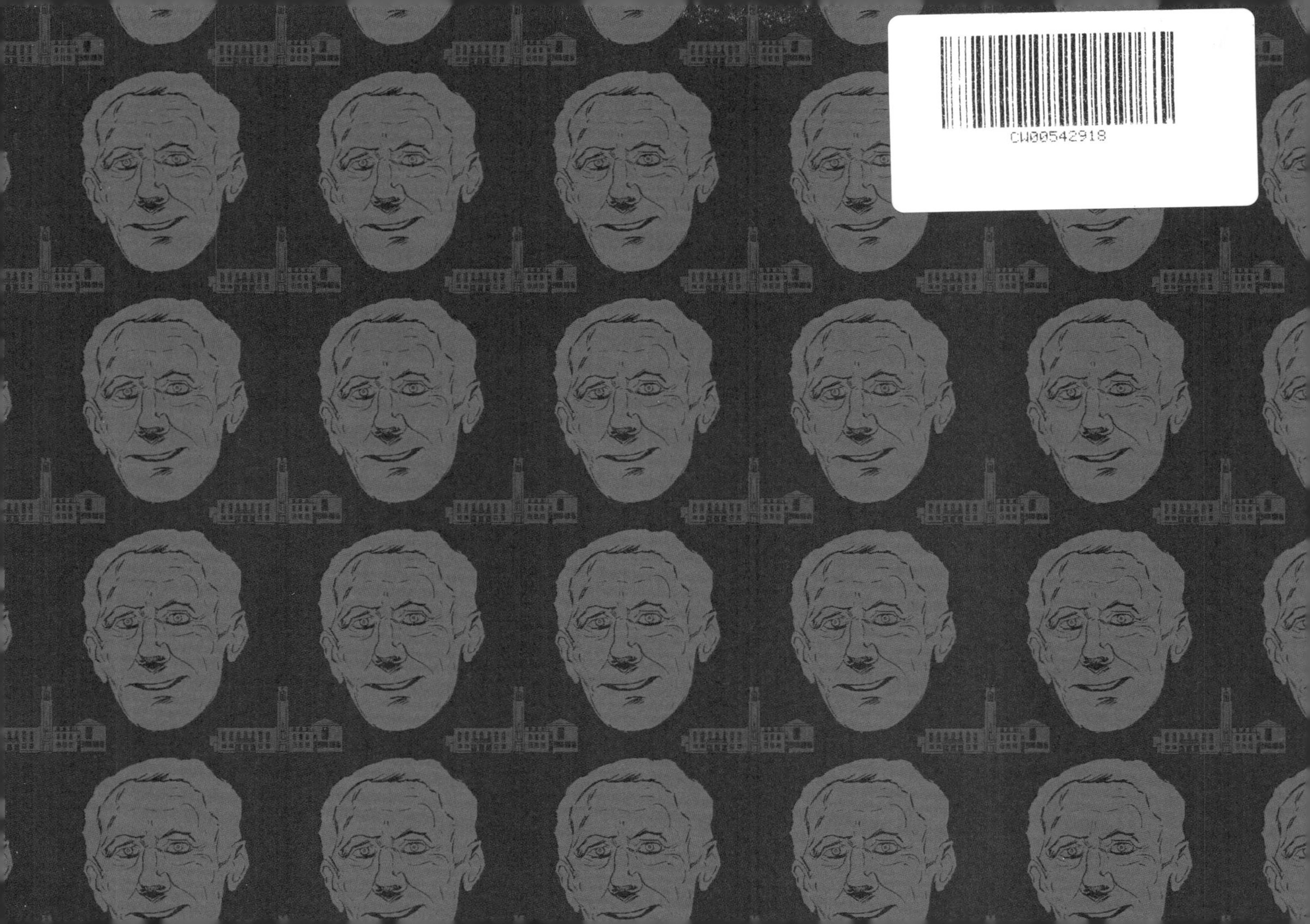

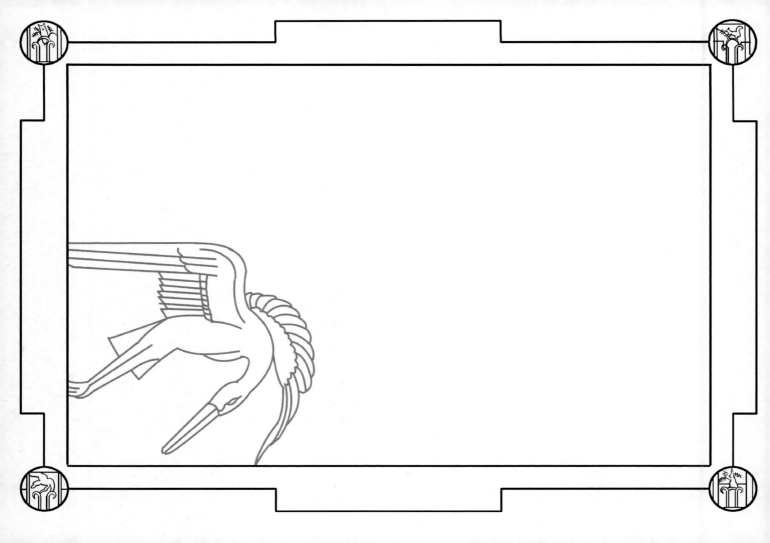

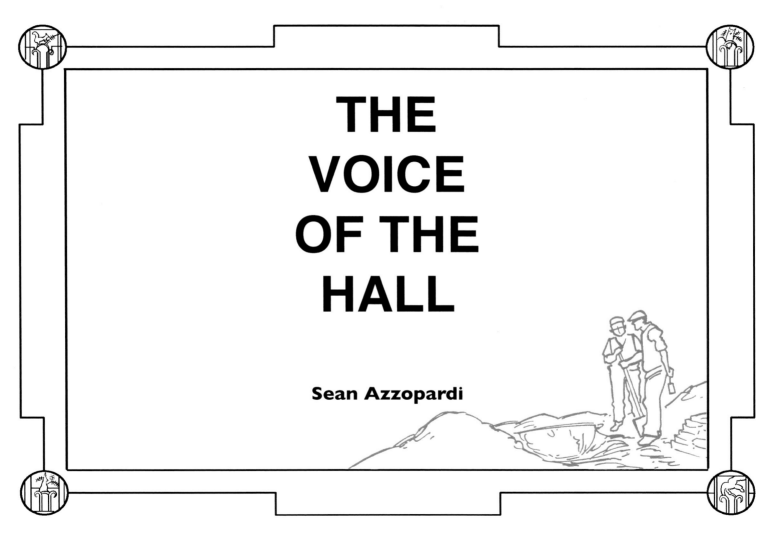

THE VOICE OF THE HALL

Sean Azzopardi

The Voice of the Hall
by Sean Azzopardi

Published by Soaring Penguin Press
4 Florence Terrace
London
SW15 3RU
UK
www.soaringpenguinpress.com

This edition (c) 2018 Soaring Penguin Press

ISBN 978-1-908030-29-0

Supported using public funding by

ARTS COUNCIL ENGLAND

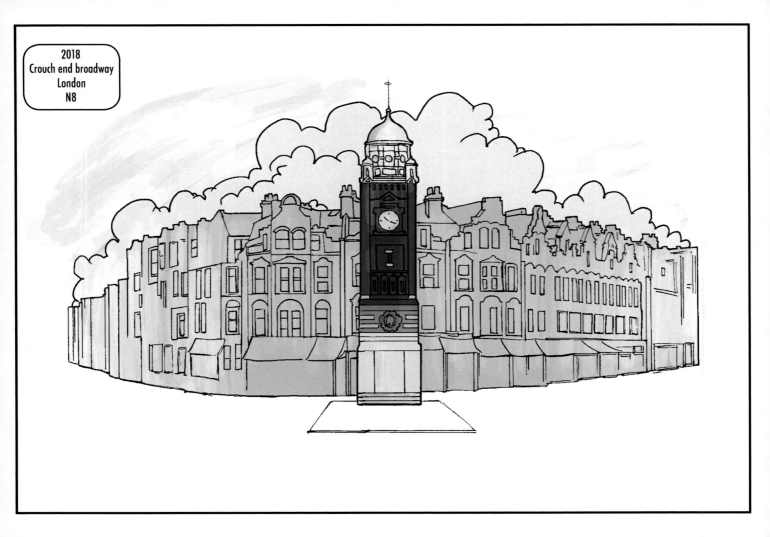

2018
Crouch end broadway
London
N8

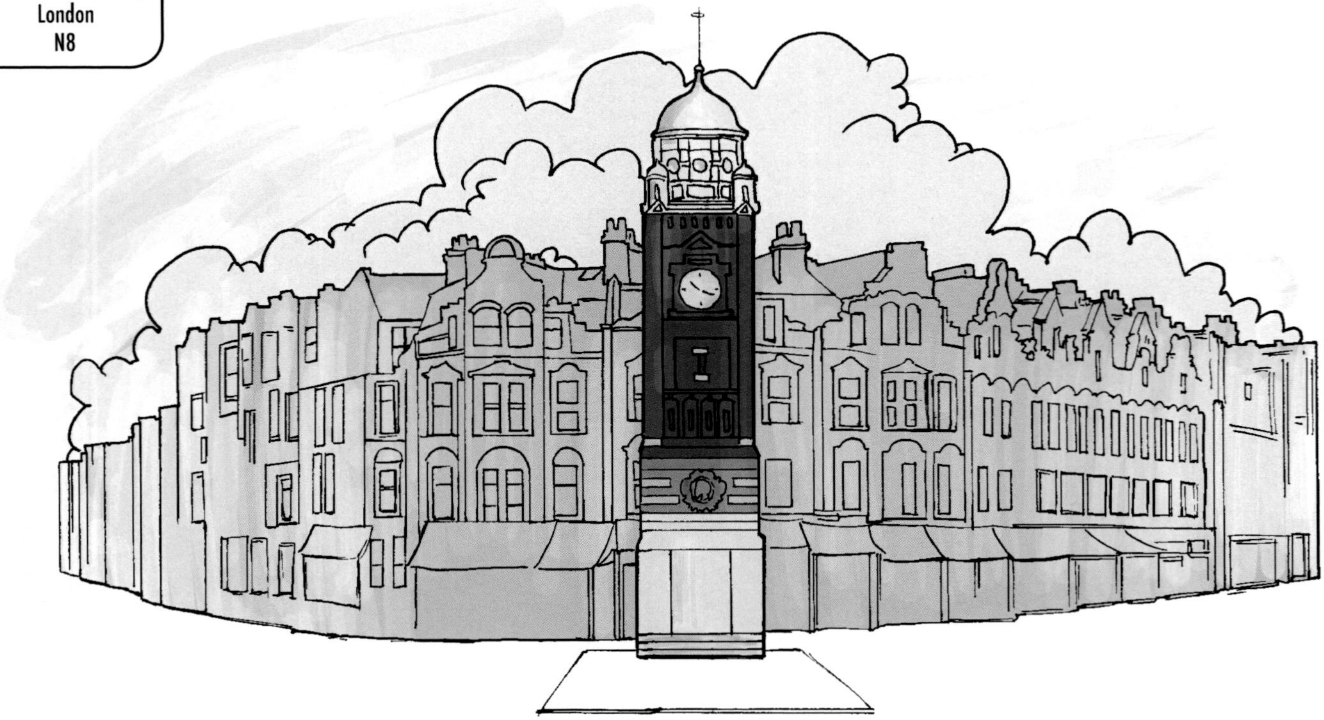

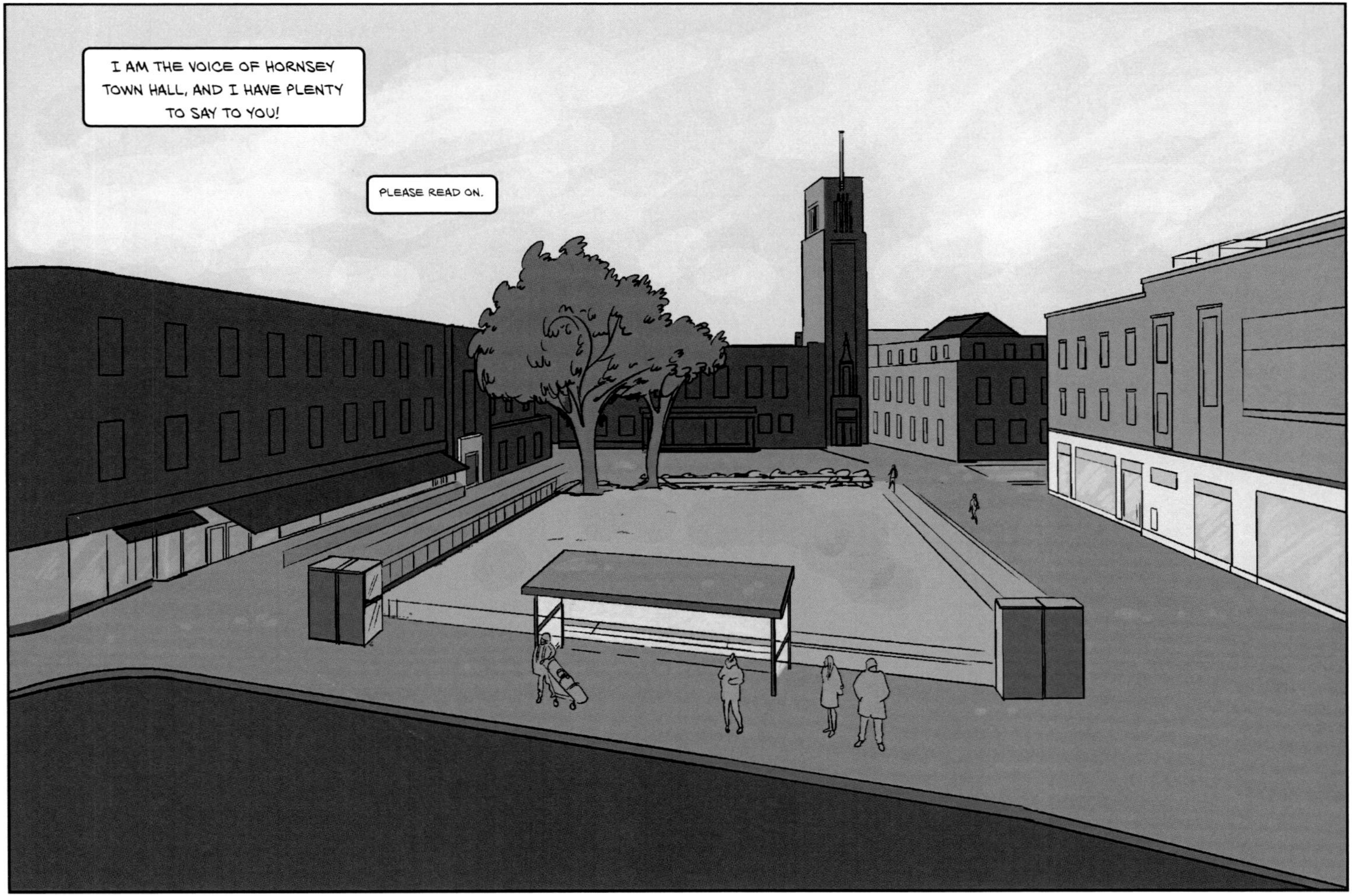
I AM THE VOICE OF HORNSEY TOWN HALL, AND I HAVE PLENTY TO SAY TO YOU!
PLEASE READ ON.

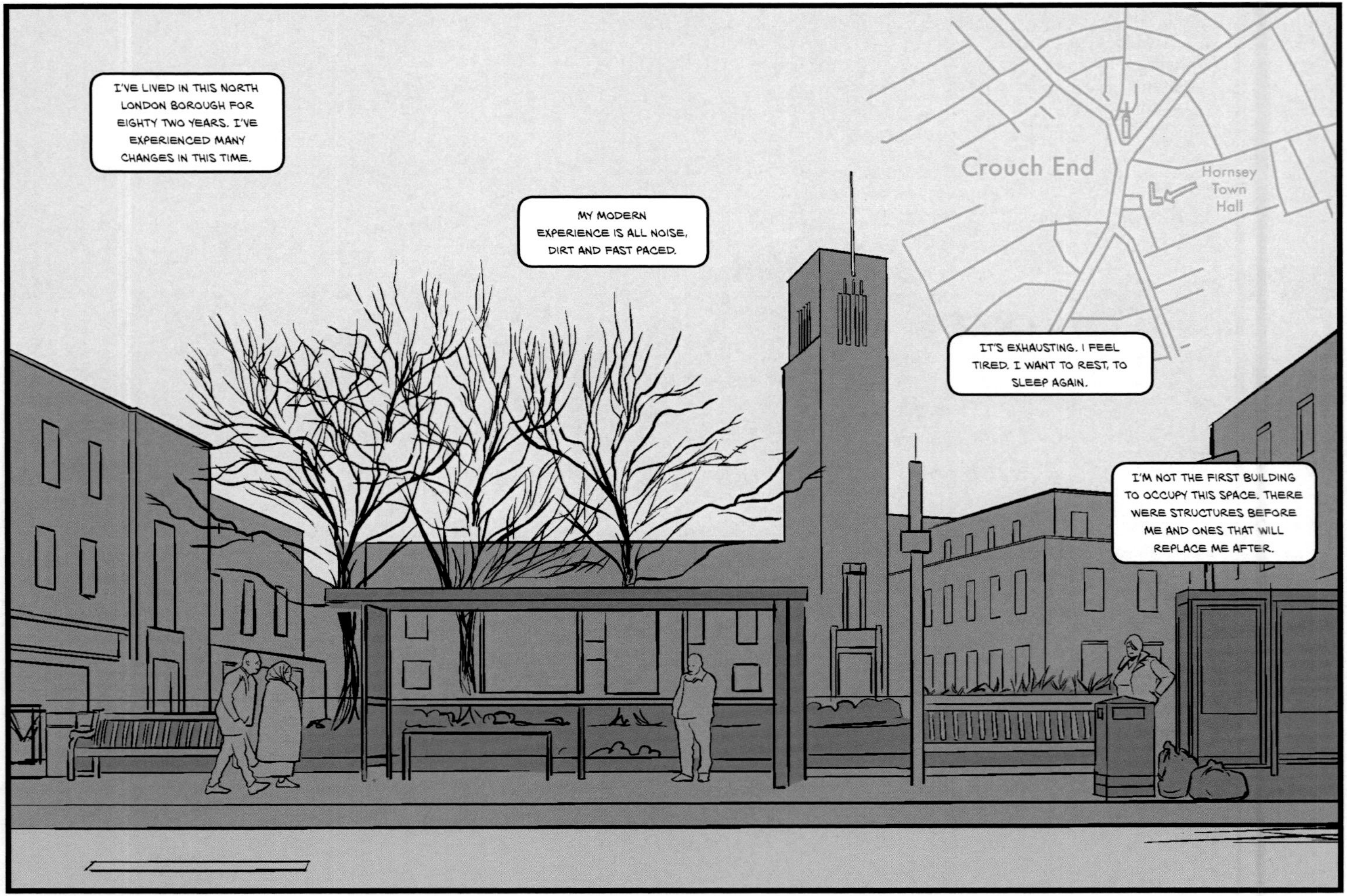

I'VE LIVED IN THIS NORTH LONDON BOROUGH FOR EIGHTY TWO YEARS. I'VE EXPERIENCED MANY CHANGES IN THIS TIME.
Crouch End
Hornsey Town Hall
MY MODERN EXPERIENCE IS ALL NOISE, DIRT AND FAST PACED.
IT'S EXHAUSTING. I FEEL TIRED. I WANT TO REST, TO SLEEP AGAIN.
I'M NOT THE FIRST BUILDING TO OCCUPY THIS SPACE. THERE WERE STRUCTURES BEFORE ME AND ONES THAT WILL REPLACE ME AFTER.

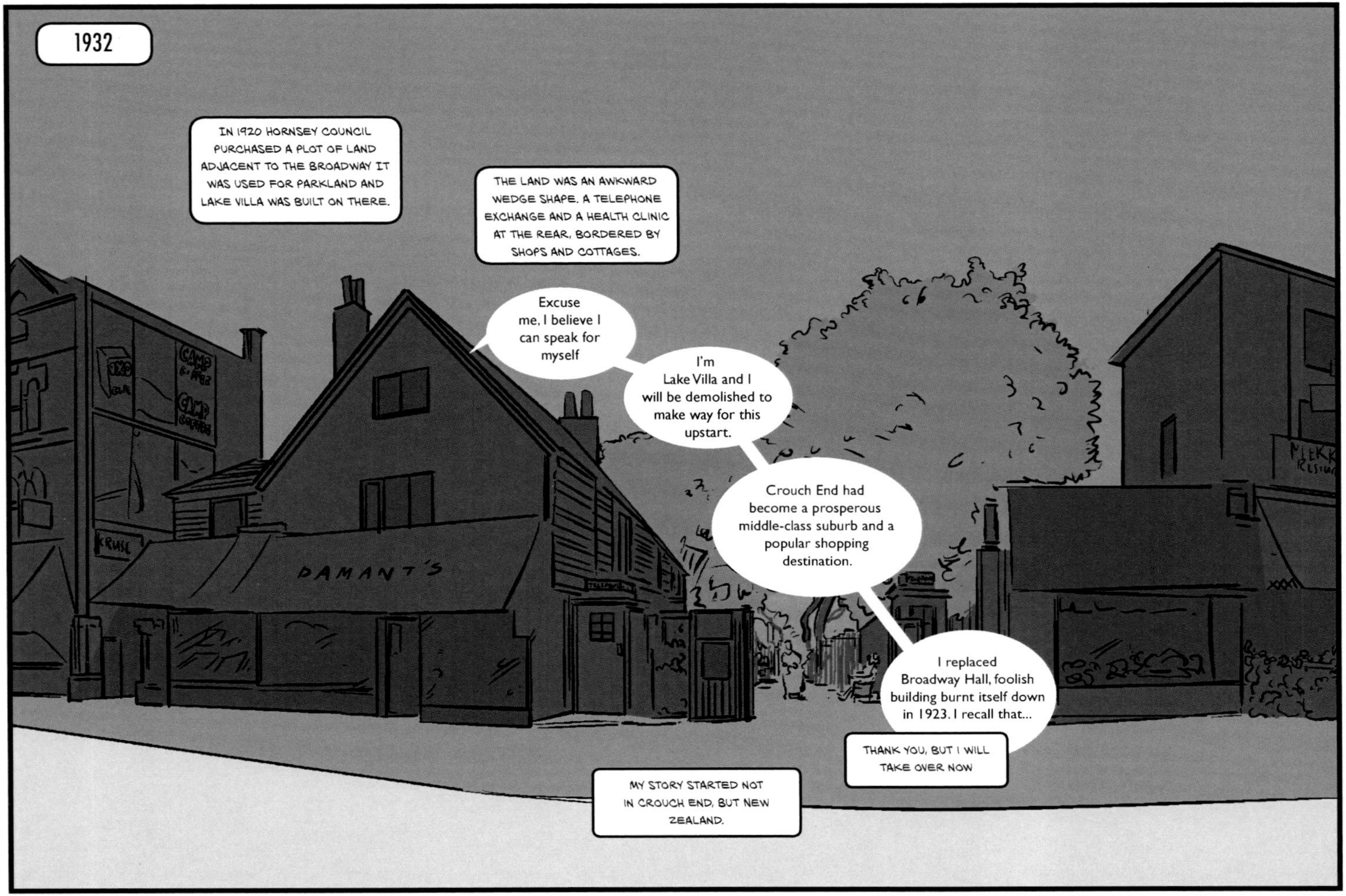
1932
IN 1920 HORNSEY COUNCIL PURCHASED A PLOT OF LAND ADJACENT TO THE BROADWAY IT WAS USED FOR PARKLAND AND LAKE VILLA WAS BUILT ON THERE.
THE LAND WAS AN AWKWARD WEDGE SHAPE. A TELEPHONE EXCHANGE AND A HEALTH CLINIC AT THE REAR, BORDERED BY SHOPS AND COTTAGES.
Excuse me, I believe I can speak for myself
I'm Lake Villa and I will be demolished to make way for this upstart.
Crouch End had become a prosperous middle-class suburb and a popular shopping destination.
I replaced Broadway Hall, foolish building burnt itself down in 1923. I recall that...
THANK YOU, BUT I WILL TAKE OVER NOW
MY STORY STARTED NOT IN CROUCH END, BUT NEW ZEALAND.
DAMANT'S
OXO
CAMP COFFEE
CAMP COFFEE

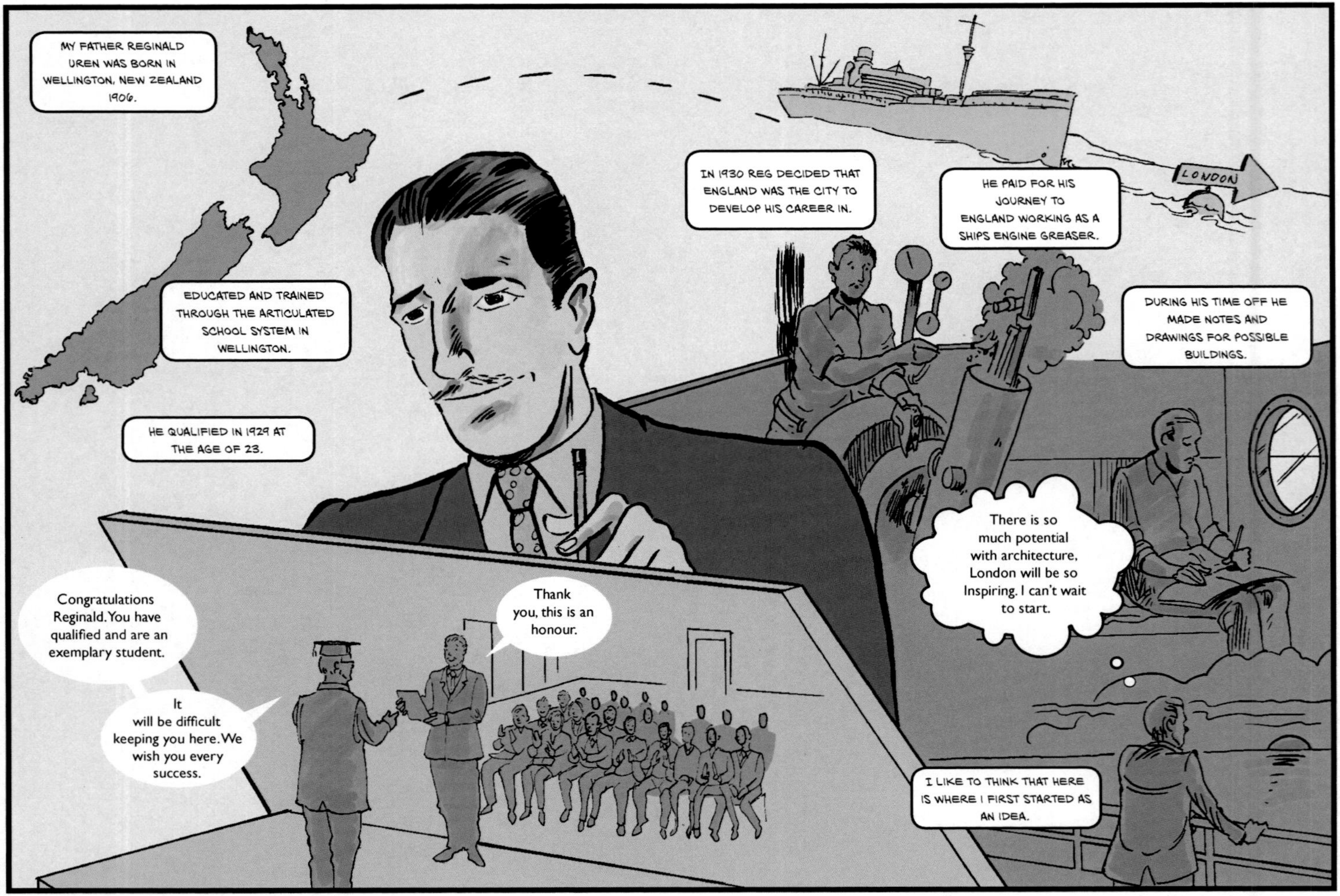

MY FATHER REGINALD UREN WAS BORN IN WELLINGTON, NEW ZEALAND 1906.
EDUCATED AND TRAINED THROUGH THE ARTICULATED SCHOOL SYSTEM IN WELLINGTON.
HE QUALIFIED IN 1929 AT THE AGE OF 23.
Congratulations Reginald. You have qualified and are an exemplary student.
Thank you, this is an honour.
It will be difficult keeping you here. We wish you every success.
IN 1930 REG DECIDED THAT ENGLAND WAS THE CITY TO DEVELOP HIS CAREER IN.
LONDON
HE PAID FOR HIS JOURNEY TO ENGLAND WORKING AS A SHIPS ENGINE GREASER.
DURING HIS TIME OFF HE MADE NOTES AND DRAWINGS FOR POSSIBLE BUILDINGS.
There is so much potential with architecture, London will be so Inspiring. I can't wait to start.
I LIKE TO THINK THAT HERE IS WHERE I FIRST STARTED AS AN IDEA.

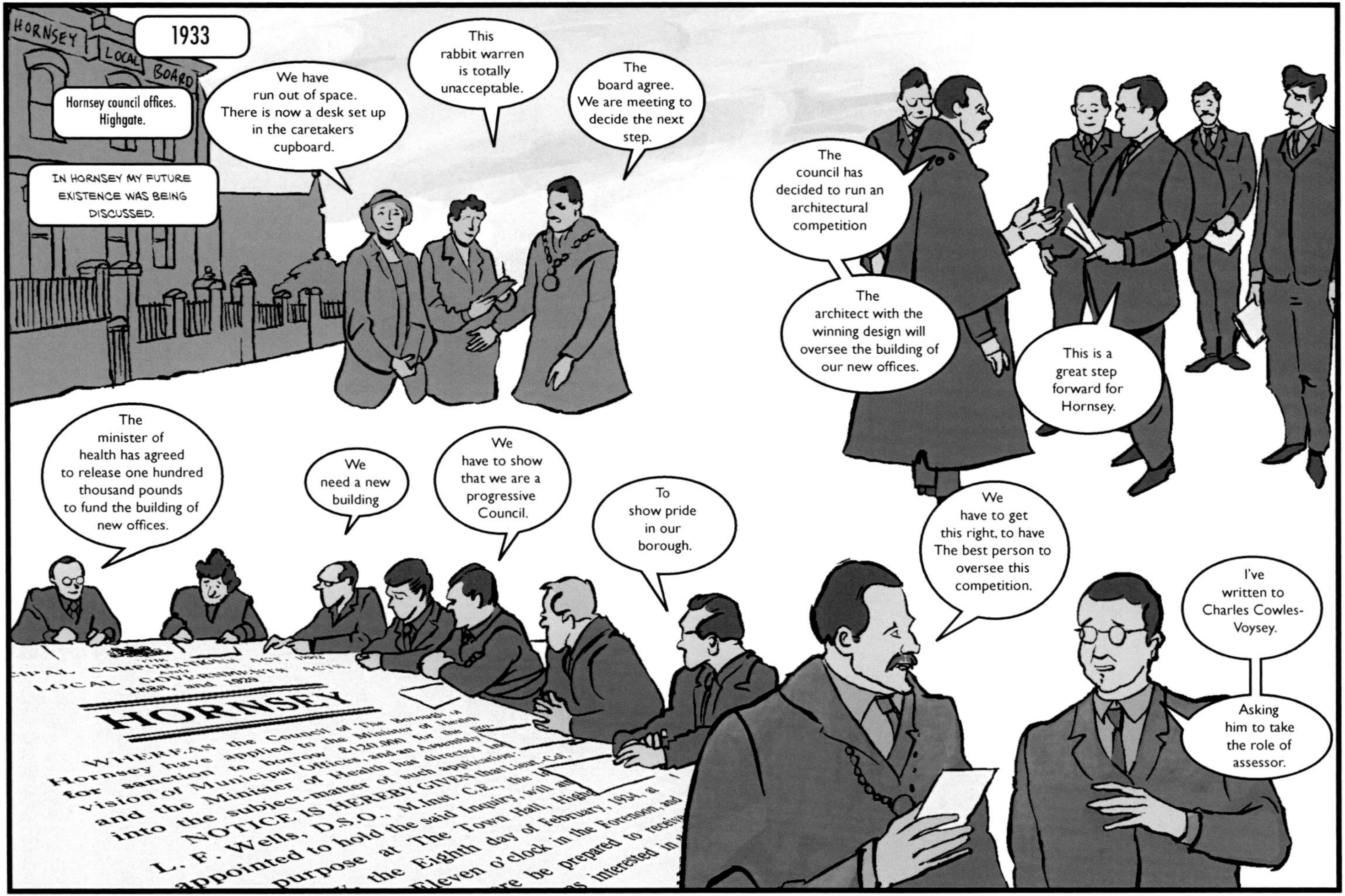
1933
HORNSEY LOCAL BOARD
Hornsey council offices. Highgate.
IN HORNSEY MY FUTURE EXISTENCE WAS BEING DISCUSSED.
We have run out of space. There is now a desk set up in the caretakers cupboard.
This rabbit warren is totally unacceptable.
The board agree. We are meeting to decide the next step.
The council has decided to run an architectural competition
The architect with the winning design will oversee the building of our new offices.
This is a great step forward for Hornsey.
The minister of health has agreed to release one hundred thousand pounds to fund the building of new offices.
We need a new building
We have to show that we are a progressive Council.
To show pride in our borough.
We have to get this right, to have The best person to oversee this competition.
I've written to Charles Cowles-Voysey.
Asking him to take the role of assessor.
HORNSEY
WHEREAS the Council of The Borough of Hornsey have applied to the Minister of Health for sanction to borrow £120,000 for the provision of Municipal Offices, and an Assembly Hall
and the Minister of Health has directed an
into the subject-matter of such application:
NOTICE IS HEREBY GIVEN that Lieut.-Col.
L. F. Wells, D.S.O., M.Inst. C.E., the
appointed to hold the said Inquiry, will at
the Eighth day of February, 1934, at
Eleven o'clock in the Forenoon, and
be prepared to receive

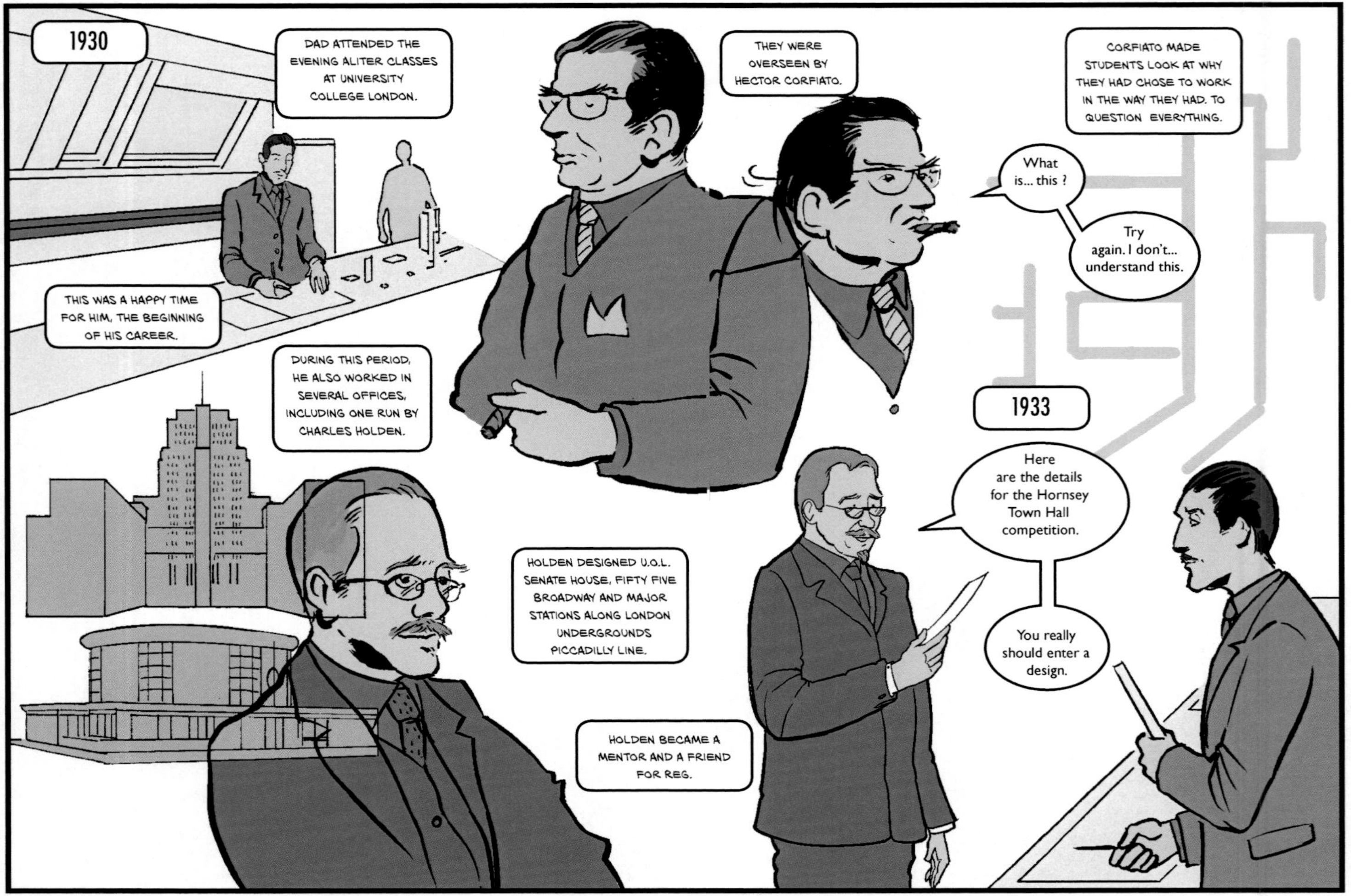
1930
DAD ATTENDED THE EVENING ALITER CLASSES AT UNIVERSITY COLLEGE LONDON.
THEY WERE OVERSEEN BY HECTOR CORFIATO.
CORFIATO MADE STUDENTS LOOK AT WHY THEY HAD CHOSE TO WORK IN THE WAY THEY HAD. TO QUESTION EVERYTHING.
What is... this ?
Try again. I don't... understand this.
THIS WAS A HAPPY TIME FOR HIM, THE BEGINNING OF HIS CAREER.
DURING THIS PERIOD, HE ALSO WORKED IN SEVERAL OFFICES, INCLUDING ONE RUN BY CHARLES HOLDEN.
1933
Here are the details for the Hornsey Town Hall competition.
You really should enter a design.
HOLDEN DESIGNED U.O.L. SENATE HOUSE, FIFTY FIVE BROADWAY AND MAJOR STATIONS ALONG LONDON UNDERGROUNDS PICCADILLY LINE.
HOLDEN BECAME A MENTOR AND A FRIEND FOR REG.

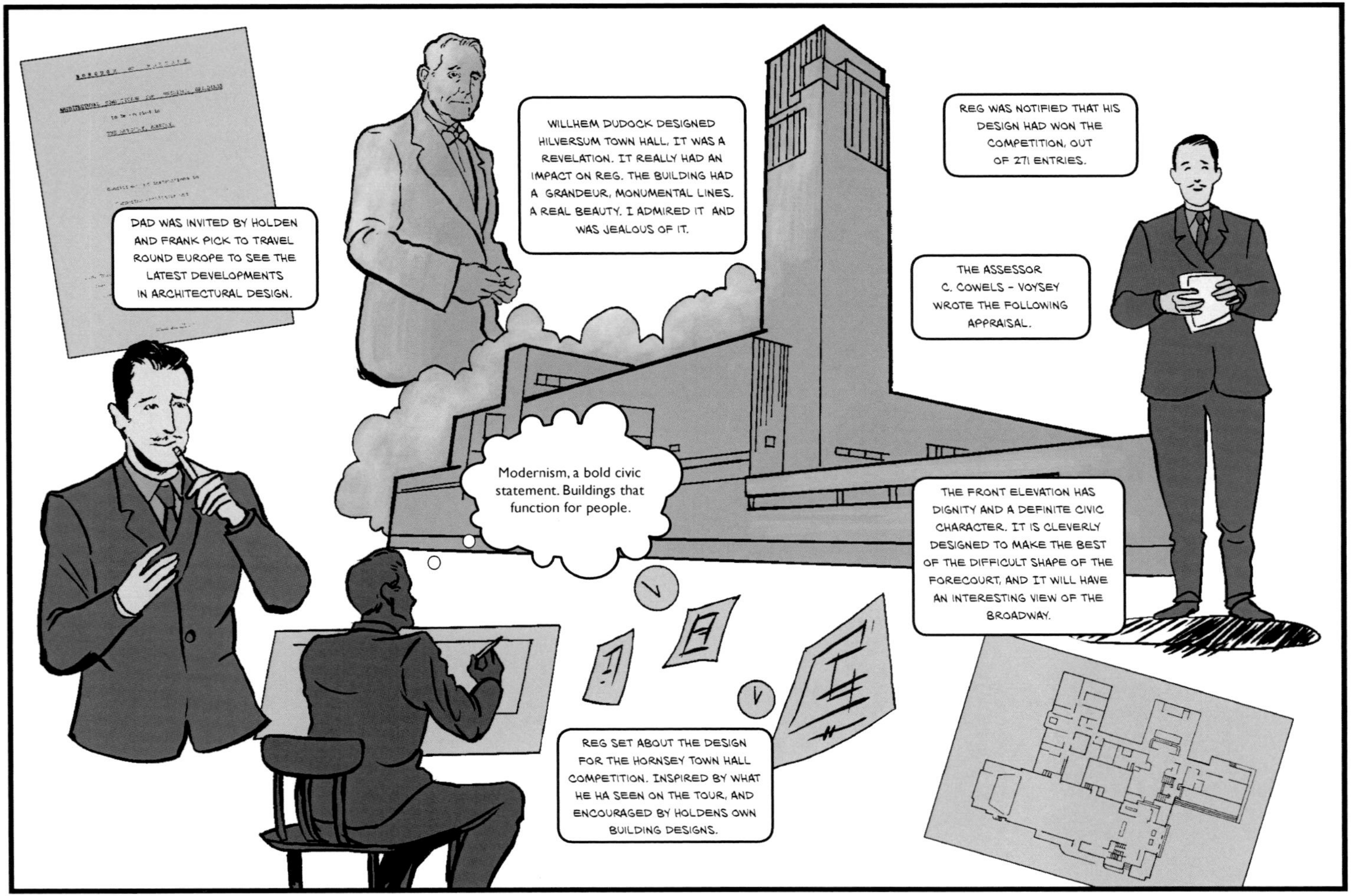
DAD WAS INVITED BY HOLDEN AND FRANK PICK TO TRAVEL ROUND EUROPE TO SEE THE LATEST DEVELOPMENTS IN ARCHITECTURAL DESIGN.
WILLHEM DUDOCK DESIGNED HILVERSUM TOWN HALL, IT WAS A REVELATION. IT REALLY HAD AN IMPACT ON REG. THE BUILDING HAD A GRANDEUR, MONUMENTAL LINES. A REAL BEAUTY. I ADMIRED IT AND WAS JEALOUS OF IT.
Modernism, a bold civic statement. Buildings that function for people.
REG SET ABOUT THE DESIGN FOR THE HORNSEY TOWN HALL COMPETITION. INSPIRED BY WHAT HE HA SEEN ON THE TOUR, AND ENCOURAGED BY HOLDENS OWN BUILDING DESIGNS.
REG WAS NOTIFIED THAT HIS DESIGN HAD WON THE COMPETITION, OUT OF 271 ENTRIES.
THE ASSESSOR C. COWELS - VOYSEY WROTE THE FOLLOWING APPRAISAL.
THE FRONT ELEVATION HAS DIGNITY AND A DEFINITE CIVIC CHARACTER. IT IS CLEVERLY DESIGNED TO MAKE THE BEST OF THE DIFFICULT SHAPE OF THE FORECOURT, AND IT WILL HAVE AN INTERESTING VIEW OF THE BROADWAY.

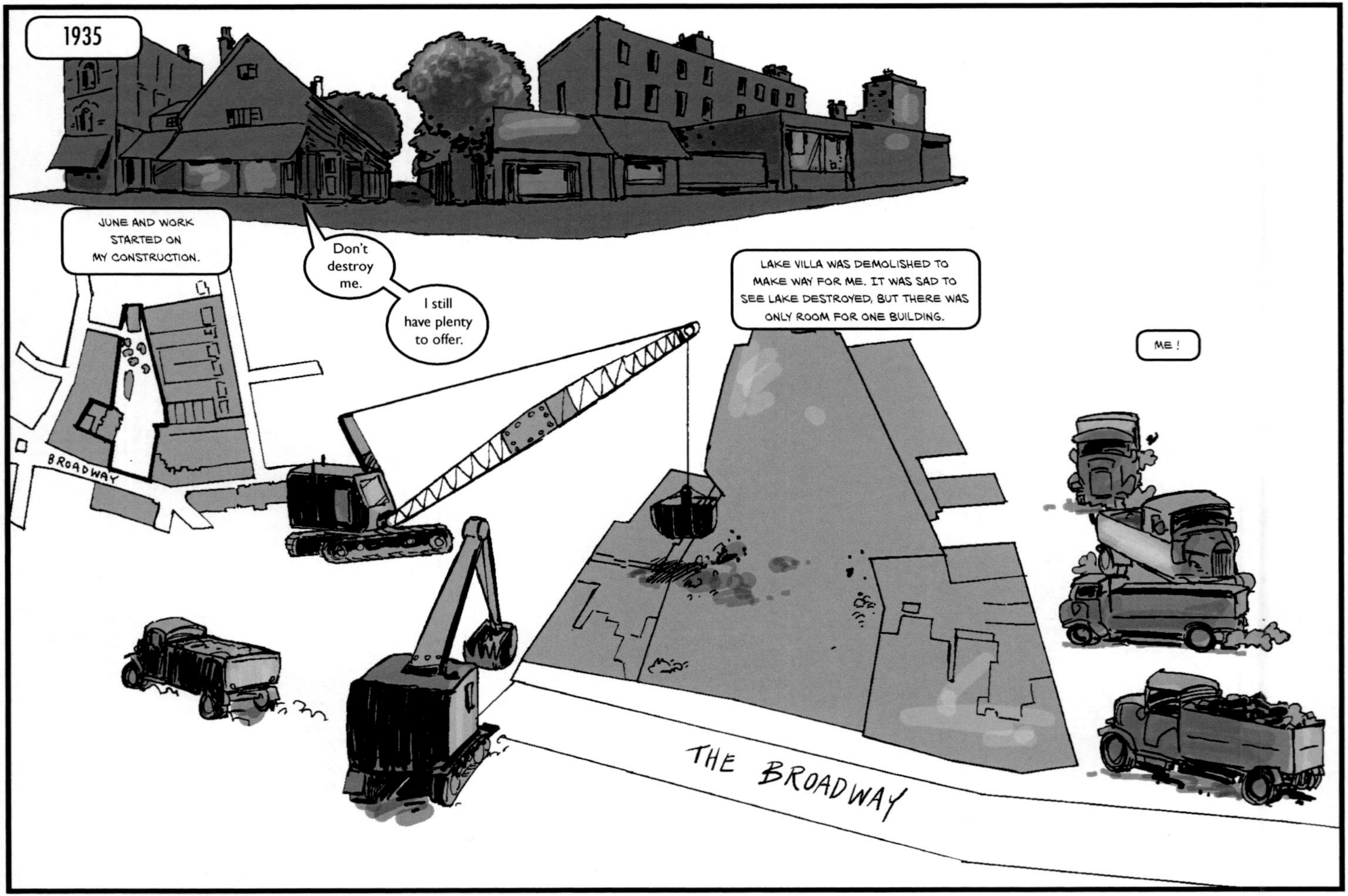
1935
JUNE AND WORK STARTED ON MY CONSTRUCTION.
Don't destroy me.
I still have plenty to offer.
LAKE VILLA WAS DEMOLISHED TO MAKE WAY FOR ME. IT WAS SAD TO SEE LAKE DESTROYED, BUT THERE WAS ONLY ROOM FOR ONE BUILDING.
ME!
BROADWAY
THE BROADWAY

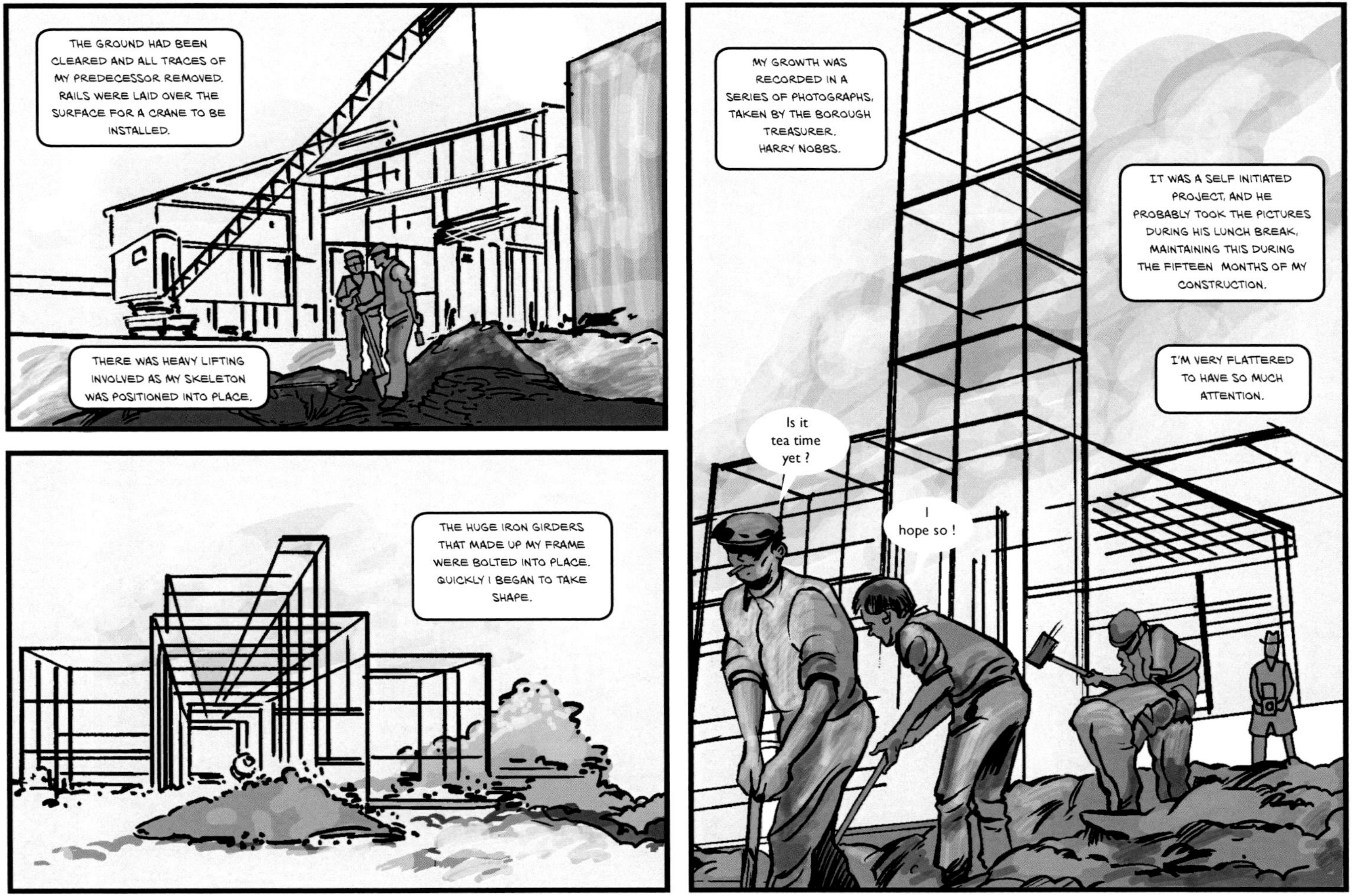

THE GROUND HAD BEEN CLEARED AND ALL TRACES OF MY PREDECESSOR REMOVED. RAILS WERE LAID OVER THE SURFACE FOR A CRANE TO BE INSTALLED.
THERE WAS HEAVY LIFTING INVOLVED AS MY SKELETON WAS POSITIONED INTO PLACE.
THE HUGE IRON GIRDERS THAT MADE UP MY FRAME WERE BOLTED INTO PLACE. QUICKLY I BEGAN TO TAKE SHAPE.
MY GROWTH WAS RECORDED IN A SERIES OF PHOTOGRAPHS, TAKEN BY THE BOROUGH TREASURER. HARRY NOBBS.
IT WAS A SELF INITIATED PROJECT, AND HE PROBABLY TOOK THE PICTURES DURING HIS LUNCH BREAK, MAINTAINING THIS DURING THE FIFTEEN MONTHS OF MY CONSTRUCTION.
I'M VERY FLATTERED TO HAVE SO MUCH ATTENTION.
Is it tea time yet ?
I hope so !

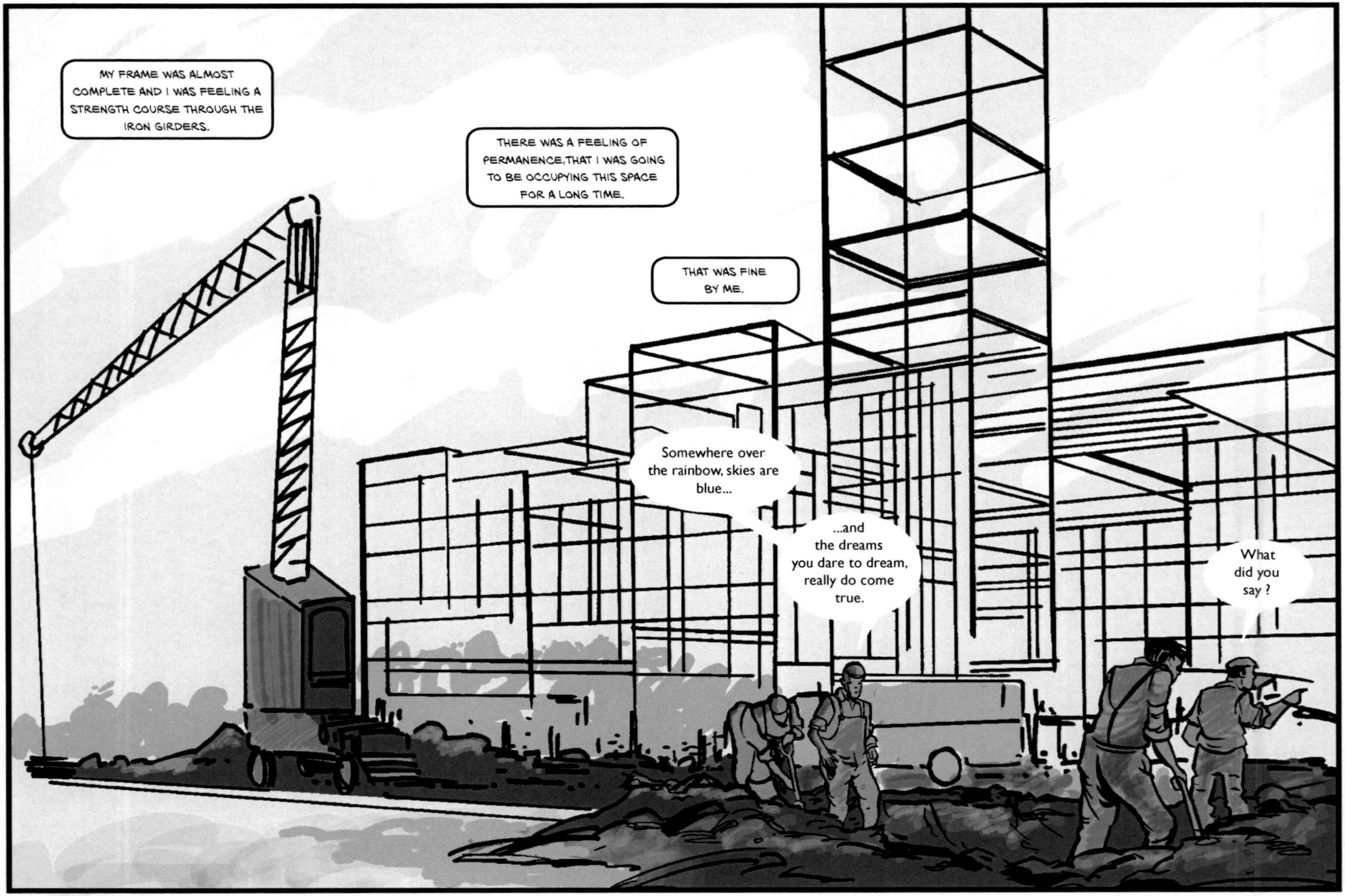
MY FRAME WAS ALMOST COMPLETE AND I WAS FEELING A STRENGTH COURSE THROUGH THE IRON GIRDERS.
THERE WAS A FEELING OF PERMANENCE,THAT I WAS GOING TO BE OCCUPYING THIS SPACE FOR A LONG TIME.
THAT WAS FINE BY ME.
Somewhere over the rainbow, skies are blue...
...and the dreams you dare to dream, really do come true.
What did you say ?

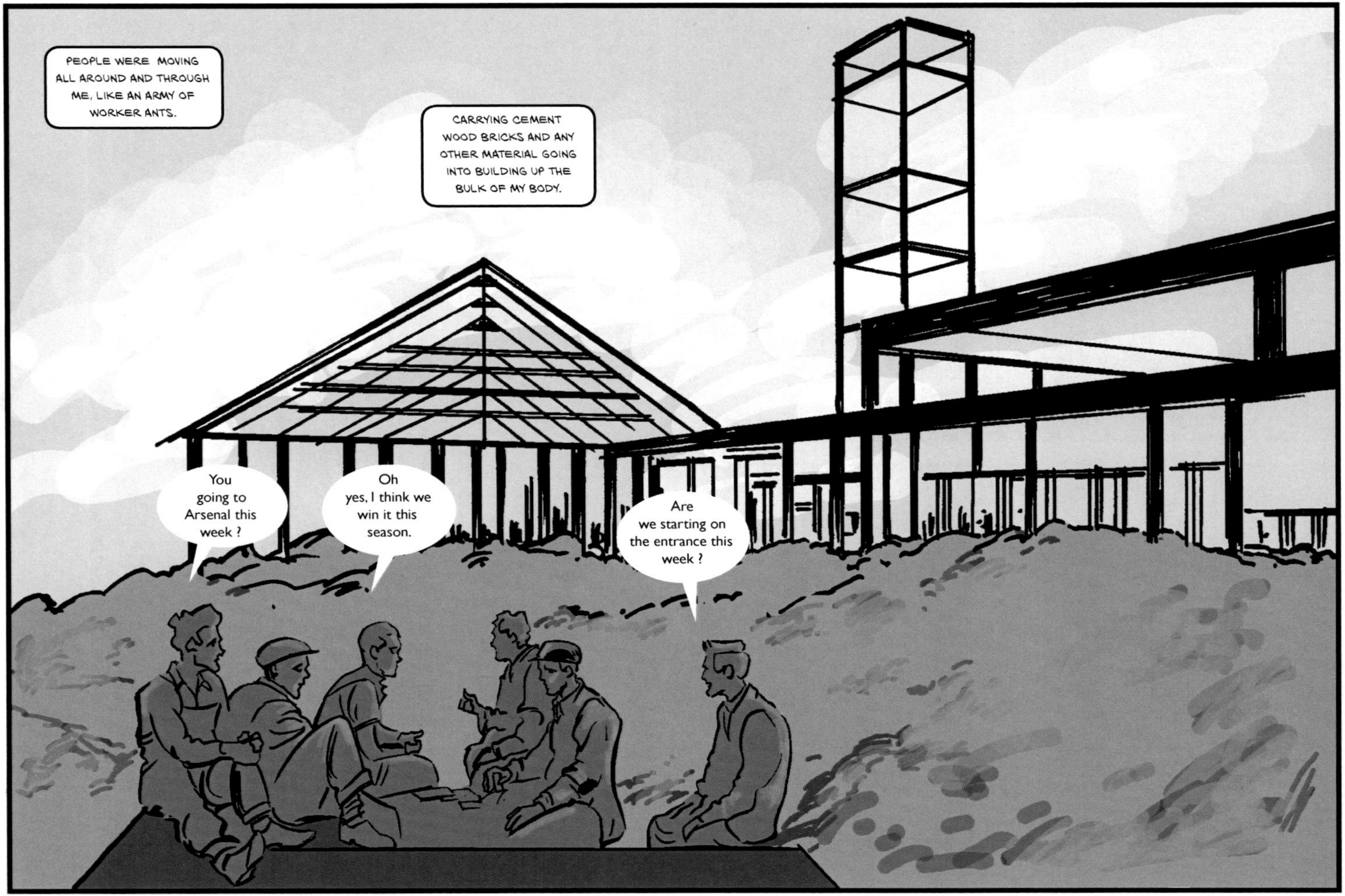
PEOPLE WERE MOVING ALL AROUND AND THROUGH ME, LIKE AN ARMY OF WORKER ANTS.
CARRYING CEMENT WOOD BRICKS AND ANY OTHER MATERIAL GOING INTO BUILDING UP THE BULK OF MY BODY.
You going to Arsenal this week ?
Oh yes, I think we win it this season.
Are we starting on the entrance this week ?

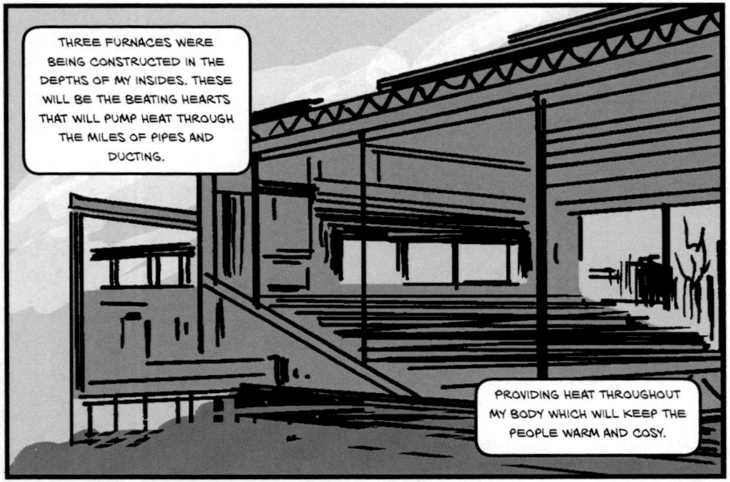
THREE FURNACES WERE BEING CONSTRUCTED IN THE DEPTHS OF MY INSIDES. THESE WILL BE THE BEATING HEARTS THAT WILL PUMP HEAT THROUGH THE MILES OF PIPES AND DUCTING.
PROVIDING HEAT THROUGHOUT MY BODY WHICH WILL KEEP THE PEOPLE WARM AND COSY.

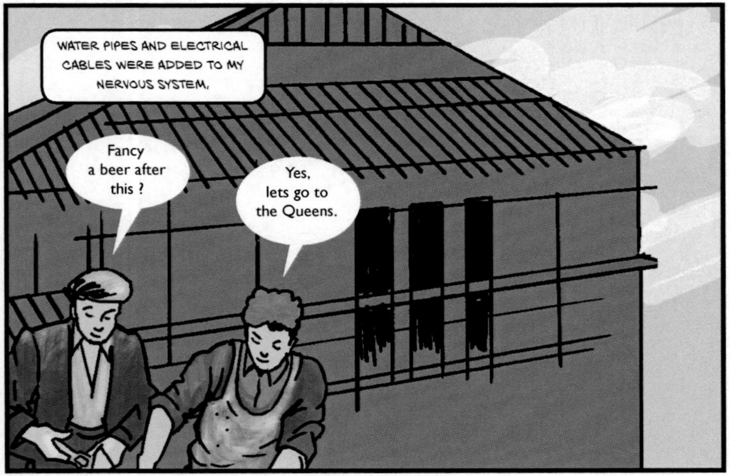
WATER PIPES AND ELECTRICAL CABLES WERE ADDED TO MY NERVOUS SYSTEM,
Fancy a beer after this ?
Yes, lets go to the Queens.

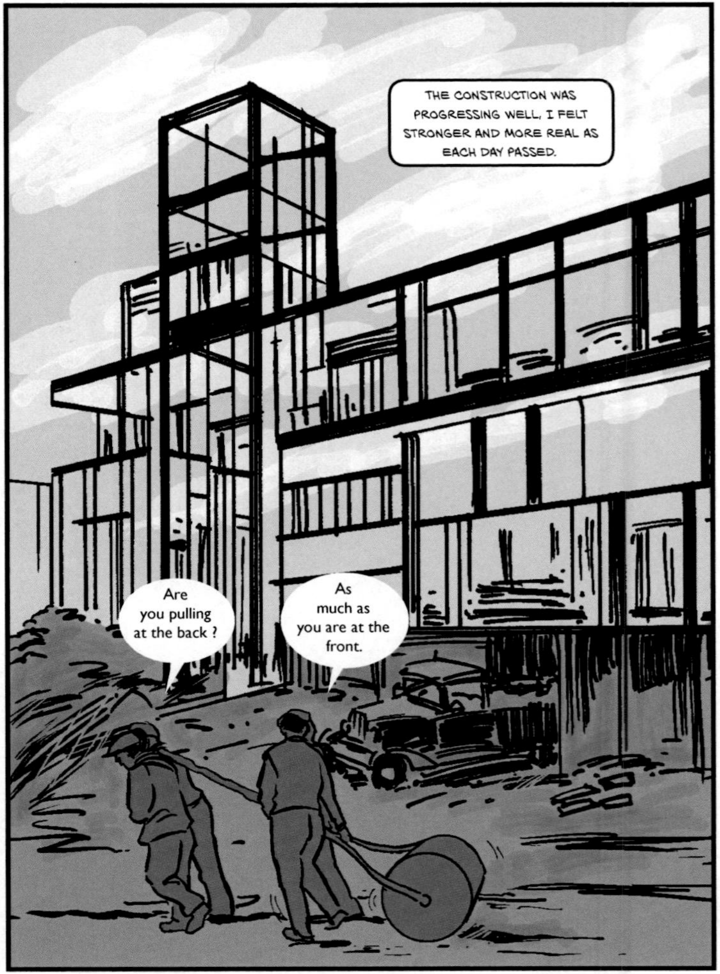
THE CONSTRUCTION WAS PROGRESSING WELL, I FELT STRONGER AND MORE REAL AS EACH DAY PASSED.
Are you pulling at the back ?
As much as you are at the front.

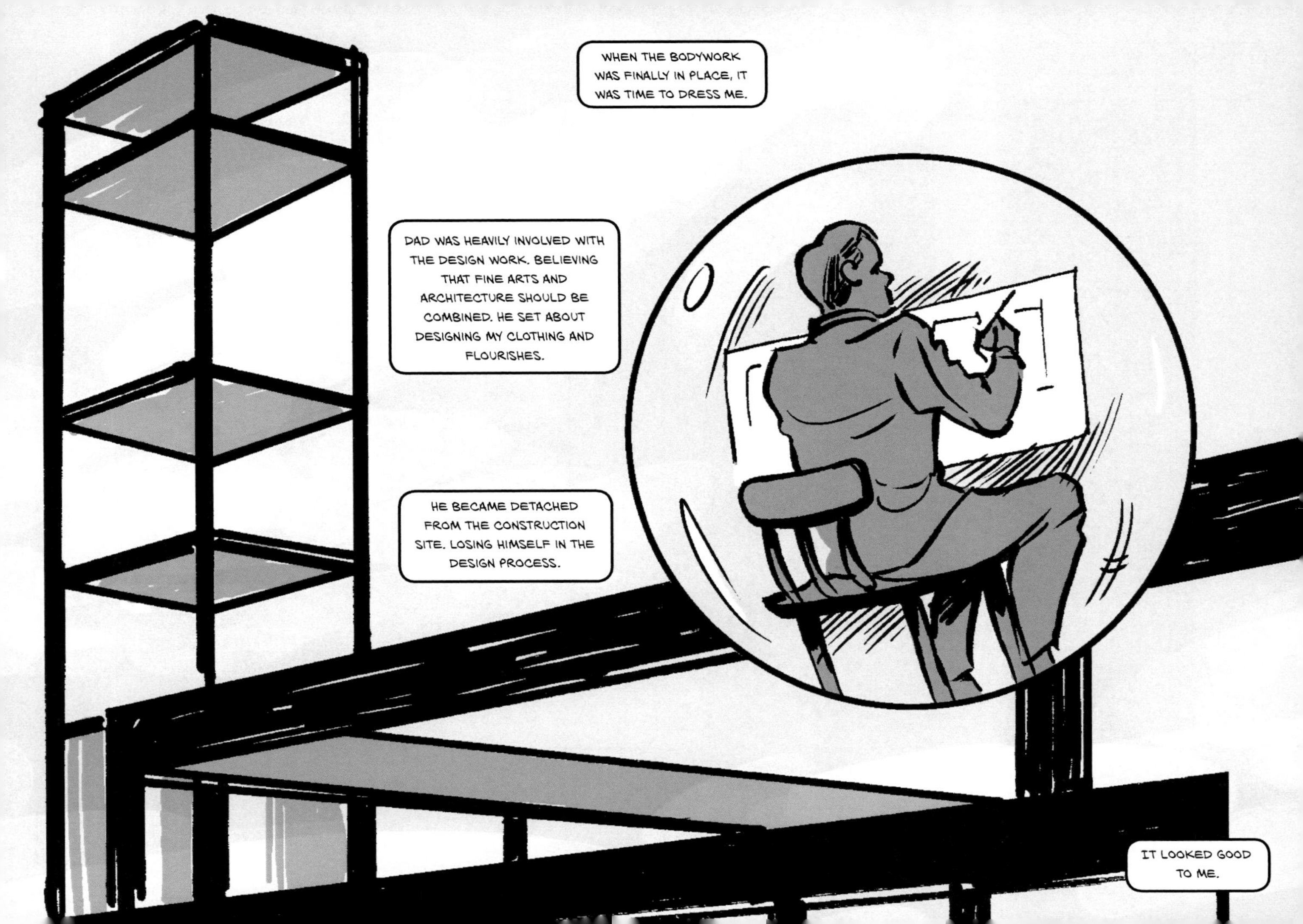
WHEN THE BODYWORK WAS FINALLY IN PLACE, IT WAS TIME TO DRESS ME.
DAD WAS HEAVILY INVOLVED WITH THE DESIGN WORK. BELIEVING THAT FINE ARTS AND ARCHITECTURE SHOULD BE COMBINED. HE SET ABOUT DESIGNING MY CLOTHING AND FLOURISHES.
HE BECAME DETACHED FROM THE CONSTRUCTION SITE. LOSING HIMSELF IN THE DESIGN PROCESS.
IT LOOKED GOOD TO ME.

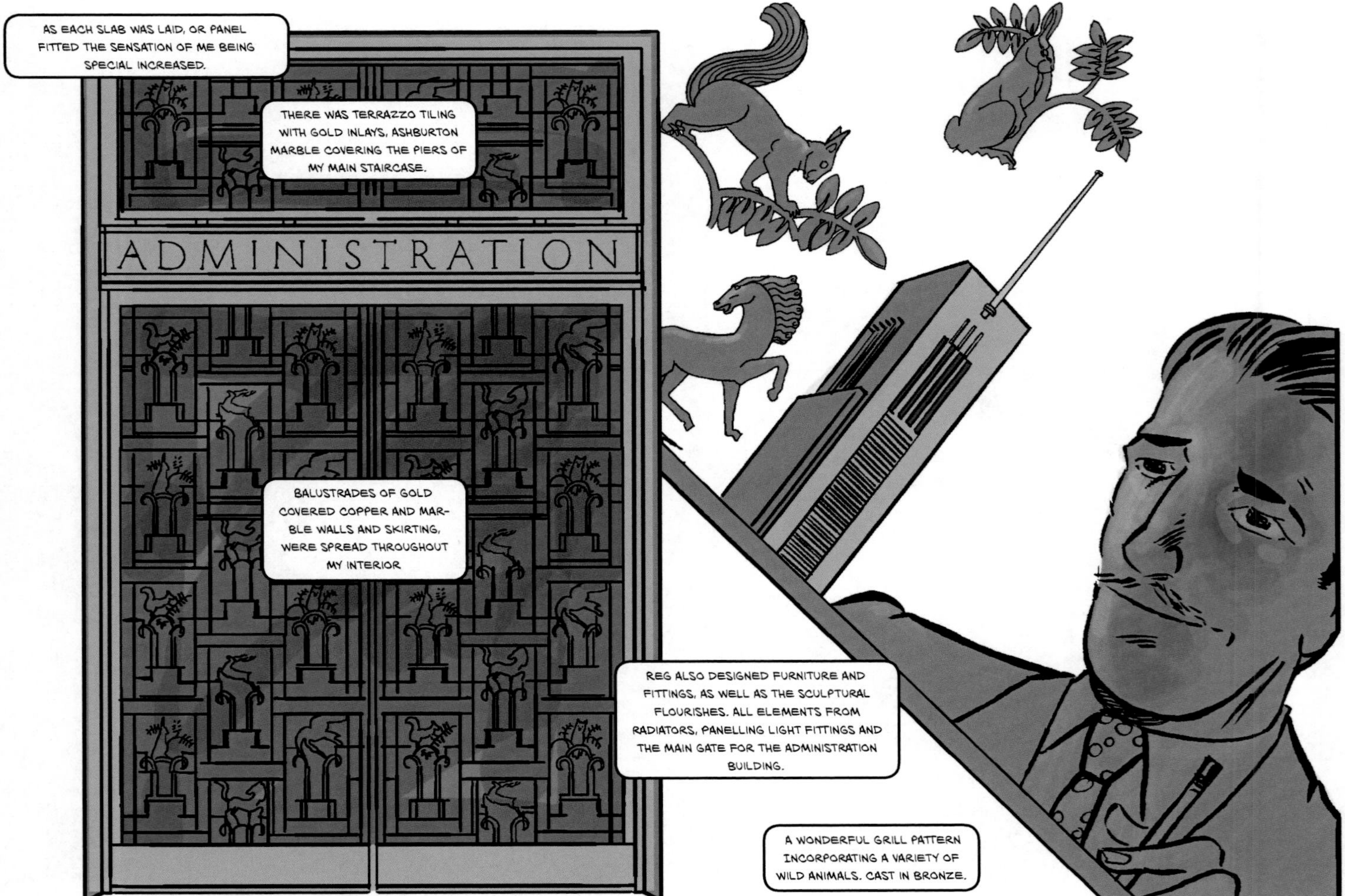
AS EACH SLAB WAS LAID, OR PANEL FITTED THE SENSATION OF ME BEING SPECIAL INCREASED.
THERE WAS TERRAZZO TILING WITH GOLD INLAYS, ASHBURTON MARBLE COVERING THE PIERS OF MY MAIN STAIRCASE.
ADMINISTRATION
BALUSTRADES OF GOLD COVERED COPPER AND MAR-BLE WALLS AND SKIRTING, WERE SPREAD THROUGHOUT MY INTERIOR
REG ALSO DESIGNED FURNITURE AND FITTINGS, AS WELL AS THE SCULPTURAL FLOURISHES. ALL ELEMENTS FROM RADIATORS, PANELLING LIGHT FITTINGS AND THE MAIN GATE FOR THE ADMINISTRATION BUILDING.
A WONDERFUL GRILL PATTERN INCORPORATING A VARIETY OF WILD ANIMALS. CAST IN BRONZE.

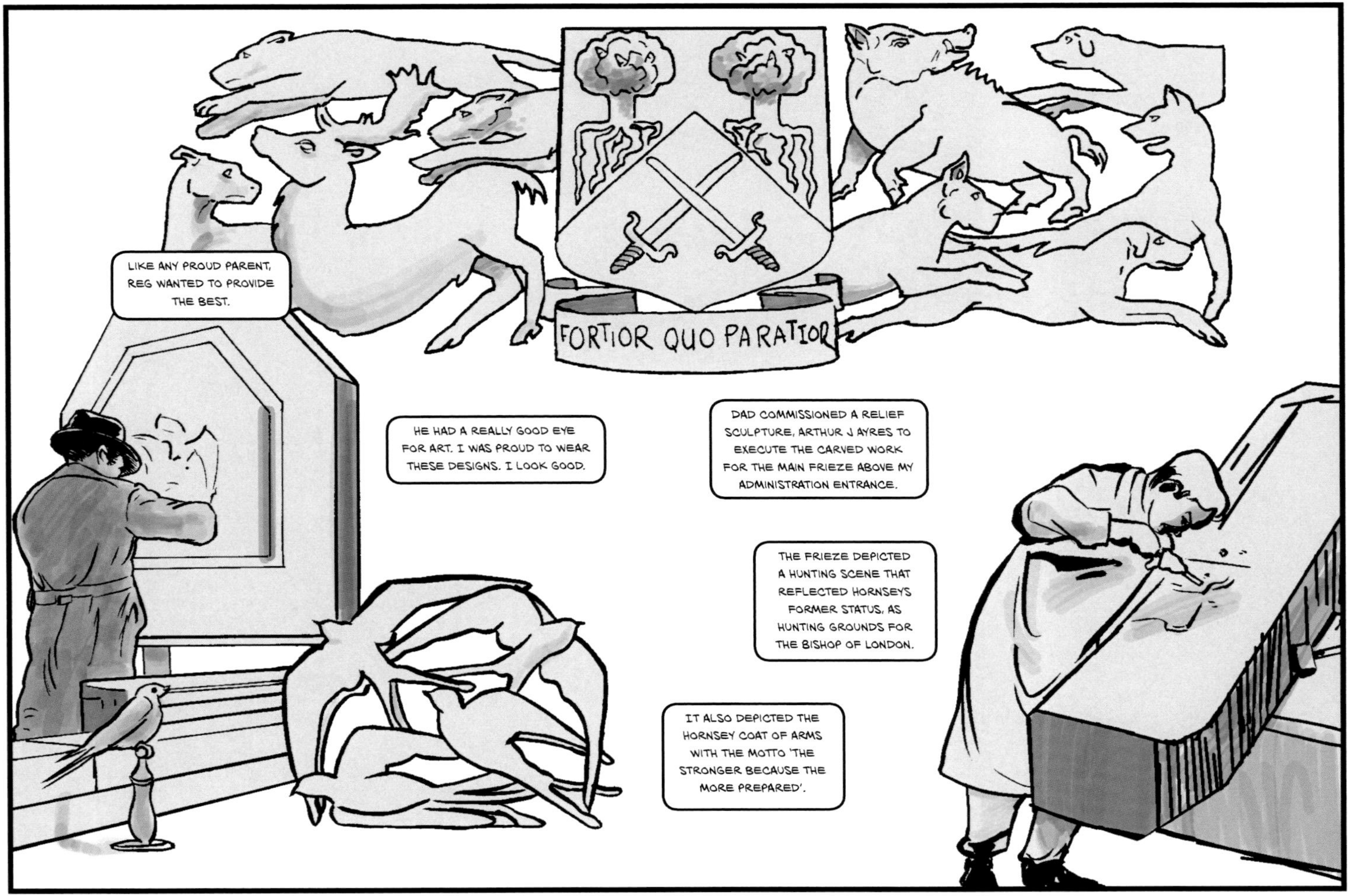
FORTIOR QUO PARATIOR
LIKE ANY PROUD PARENT, REG WANTED TO PROVIDE THE BEST.
HE HAD A REALLY GOOD EYE FOR ART. I WAS PROUD TO WEAR THESE DESIGNS. I LOOK GOOD.
DAD COMMISSIONED A RELIEF SCULPTURE, ARTHUR J AYRES TO EXECUTE THE CARVED WORK FOR THE MAIN FRIEZE ABOVE MY ADMINISTRATION ENTRANCE.
THE FRIEZE DEPICTED A HUNTING SCENE THAT REFLECTED HORNSEY'S FORMER STATUS, AS HUNTING GROUNDS FOR THE BISHOP OF LONDON.
IT ALSO DEPICTED THE HORNSEY COAT OF ARMS WITH THE MOTTO 'THE STRONGER BECAUSE THE MORE PREPARED'.

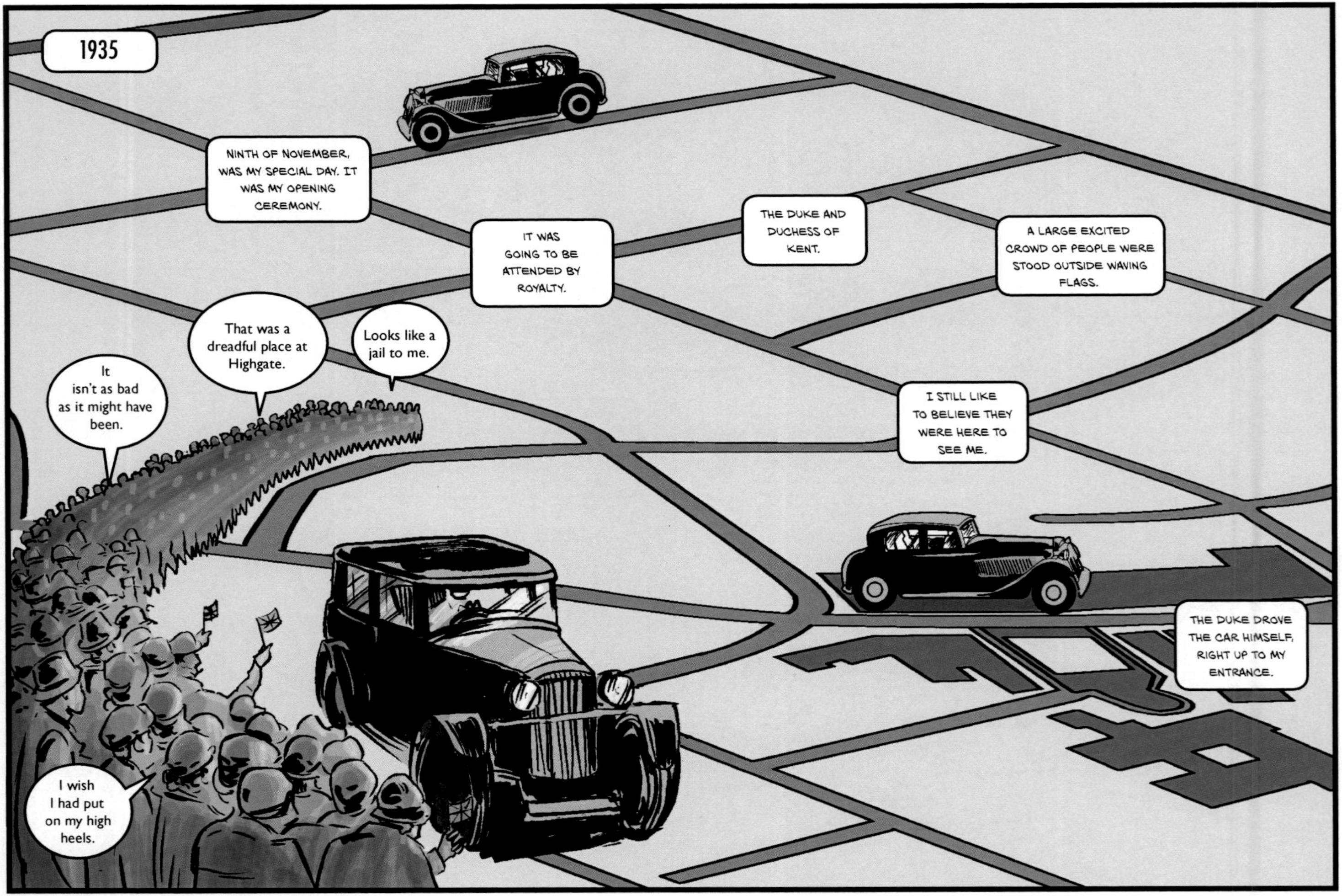

1935
NINTH OF NOVEMBER, WAS MY SPECIAL DAY. IT WAS MY OPENING CEREMONY.
IT WAS GOING TO BE ATTENDED BY ROYALTY.
THE DUKE AND DUCHESS OF KENT.
A LARGE EXCITED CROWD OF PEOPLE WERE STOOD OUTSIDE WAVING FLAGS.
It isn't as bad as it might have been.
That was a dreadful place at Highgate.
Looks like a jail to me.
I STILL LIKE TO BELIEVE THEY WERE HERE TO SEE ME.
THE DUKE DROVE THE CAR HIMSELF, RIGHT UP TO MY ENTRANCE.
I wish I had put on my high heels.

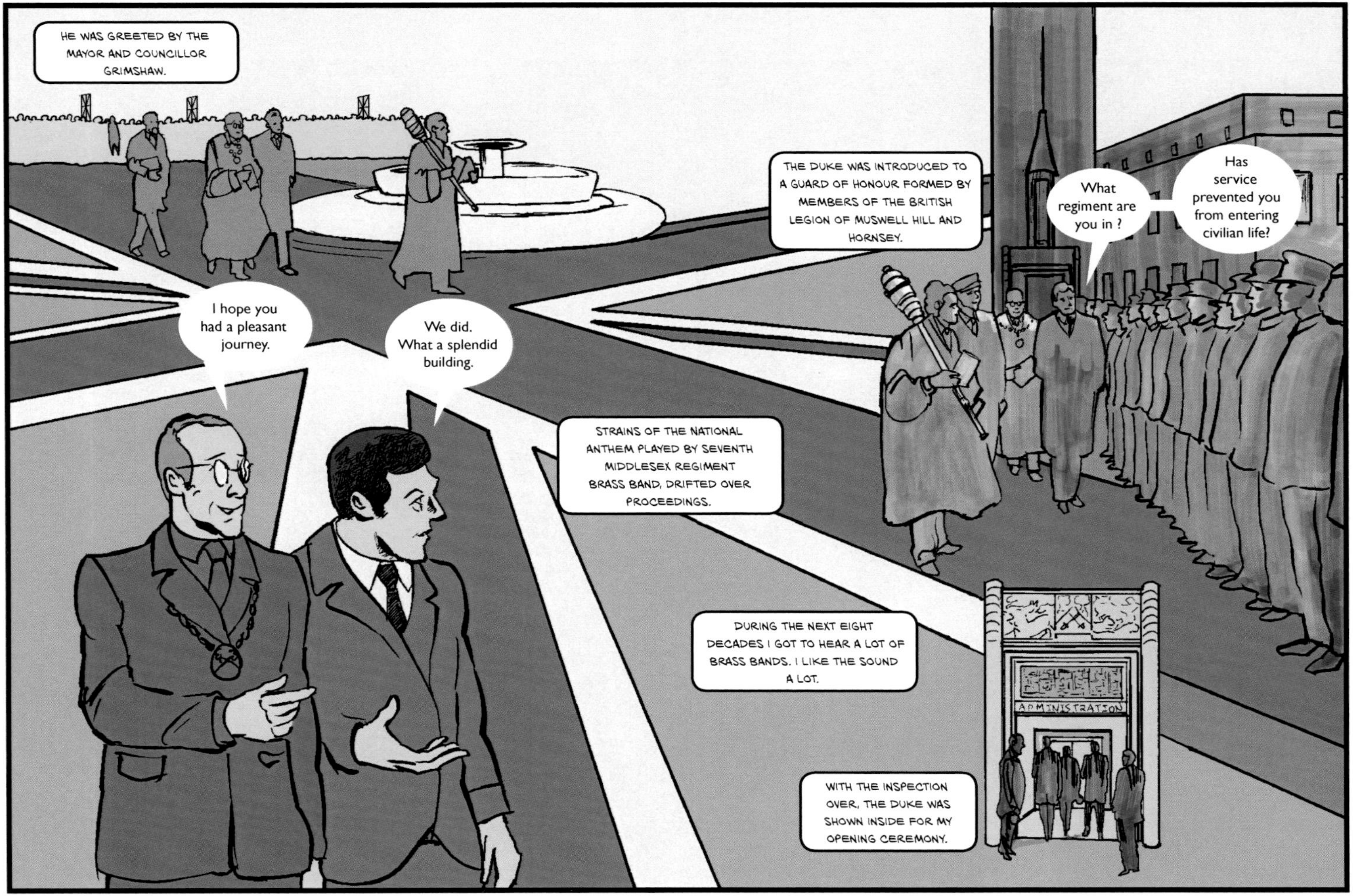
HE WAS GREETED BY THE MAYOR AND COUNCILLOR GRIMSHAW.
I hope you had a pleasant journey.
We did. What a splendid building.
STRAINS OF THE NATIONAL ANTHEM PLAYED BY SEVENTH MIDDLESEX REGIMENT BRASS BAND, DRIFTED OVER PROCEEDINGS.
THE DUKE WAS INTRODUCED TO A GUARD OF HONOUR FORMED BY MEMBERS OF THE BRITISH LEGION OF MUSWELL HILL AND HORNSEY.
What regiment are you in ?
Has service prevented you from entering civilian life?
DURING THE NEXT EIGHT DECADES I GOT TO HEAR A LOT OF BRASS BANDS. I LIKE THE SOUND A LOT.
ADMINISTRATION
WITH THE INSPECTION OVER, THE DUKE WAS SHOWN INSIDE FOR MY OPENING CEREMONY.

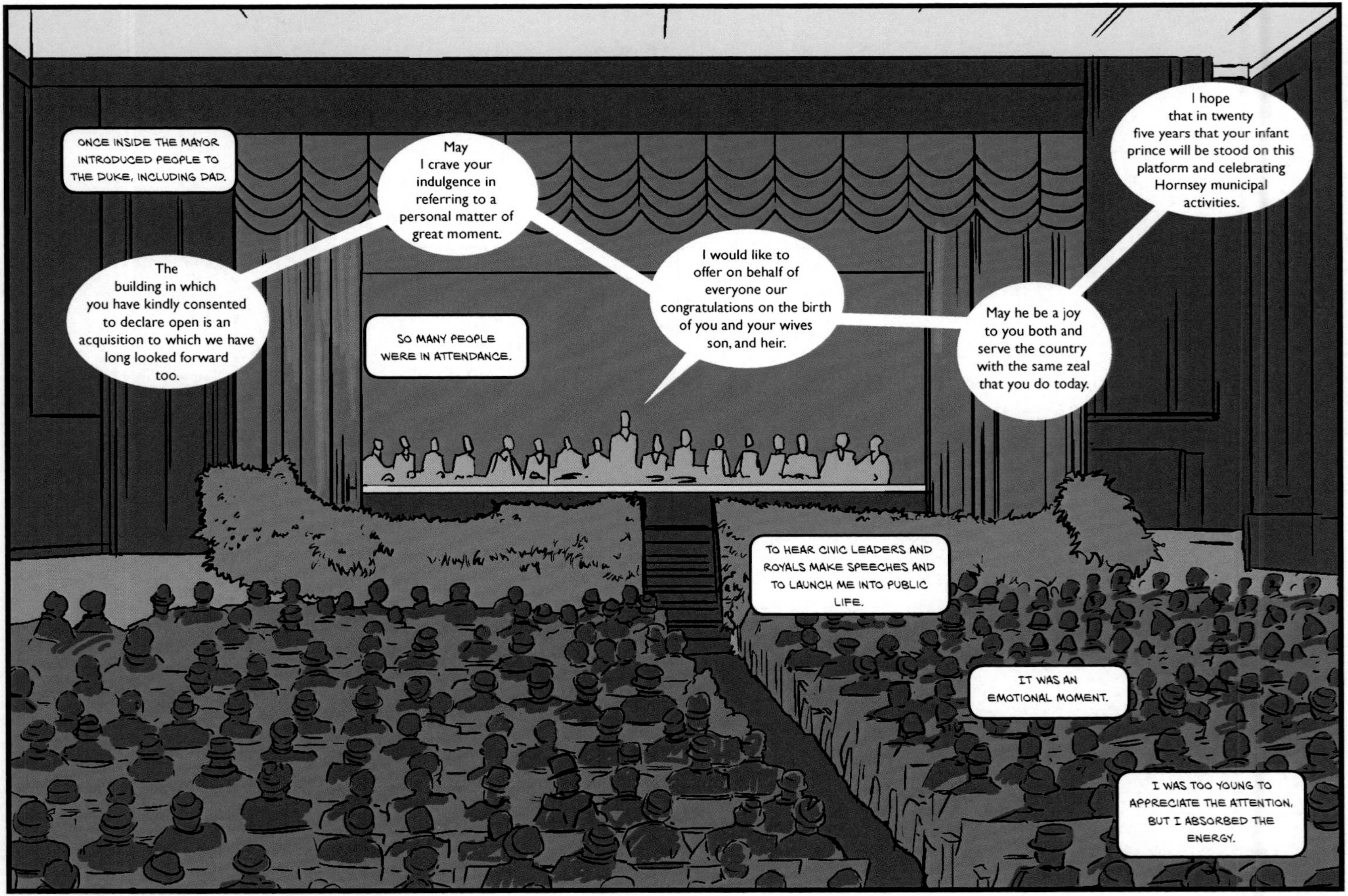

ONCE INSIDE THE MAYOR INTRODUCED PEOPLE TO THE DUKE, INCLUDING DAD.
The building in which you have kindly consented to declare open is an acquisition to which we have long looked forward too.
May I crave your indulgence in referring to a personal matter of great moment.
I would like to offer on behalf of everyone our congratulations on the birth of you and your wives son, and heir.
May he be a joy to you both and serve the country with the same zeal that you do today.
I hope that in twenty five years that your infant prince will be stood on this platform and celebrating Hornsey municipal activities.
SO MANY PEOPLE WERE IN ATTENDANCE.
TO HEAR CIVIC LEADERS AND ROYALS MAKE SPEECHES AND TO LAUNCH ME INTO PUBLIC LIFE.
IT WAS AN EMOTIONAL MOMENT.
I WAS TOO YOUNG TO APPRECIATE THE ATTENTION, BUT I ABSORBED THE ENERGY.

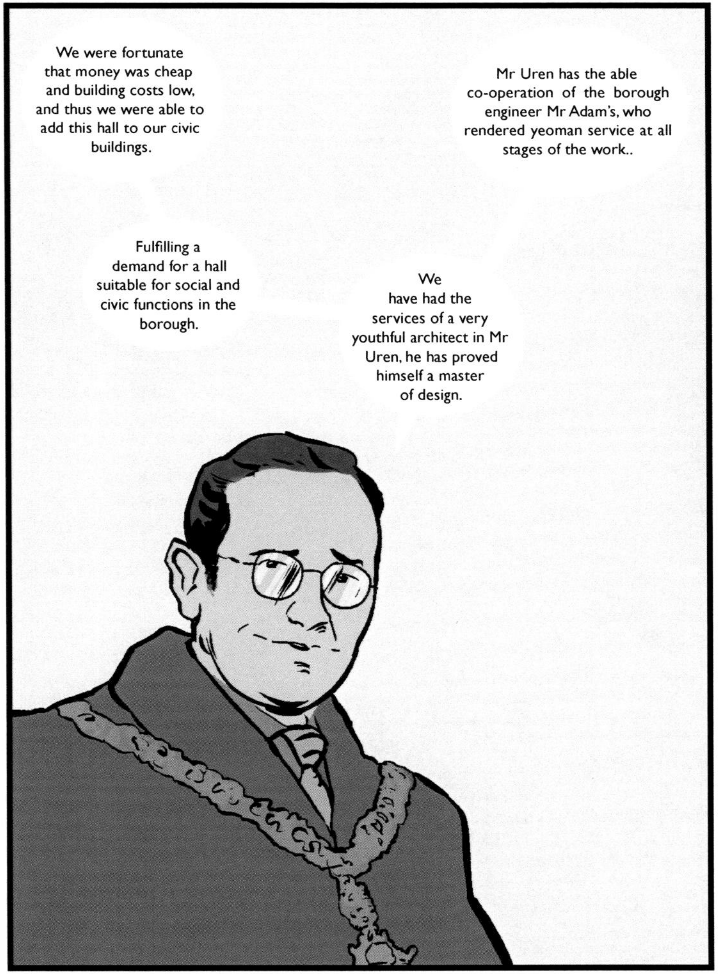
We were fortunate that money was cheap and building costs low, and thus we were able to add this hall to our civic buildings.
Mr Uren has the able co-operation of the borough engineer Mr Adam's, who rendered yeoman service at all stages of the work..
Fulfilling a demand for a hall suitable for social and civic functions in the borough.
We have had the services of a very youthful architect in Mr Uren, he has proved himself a master of design.

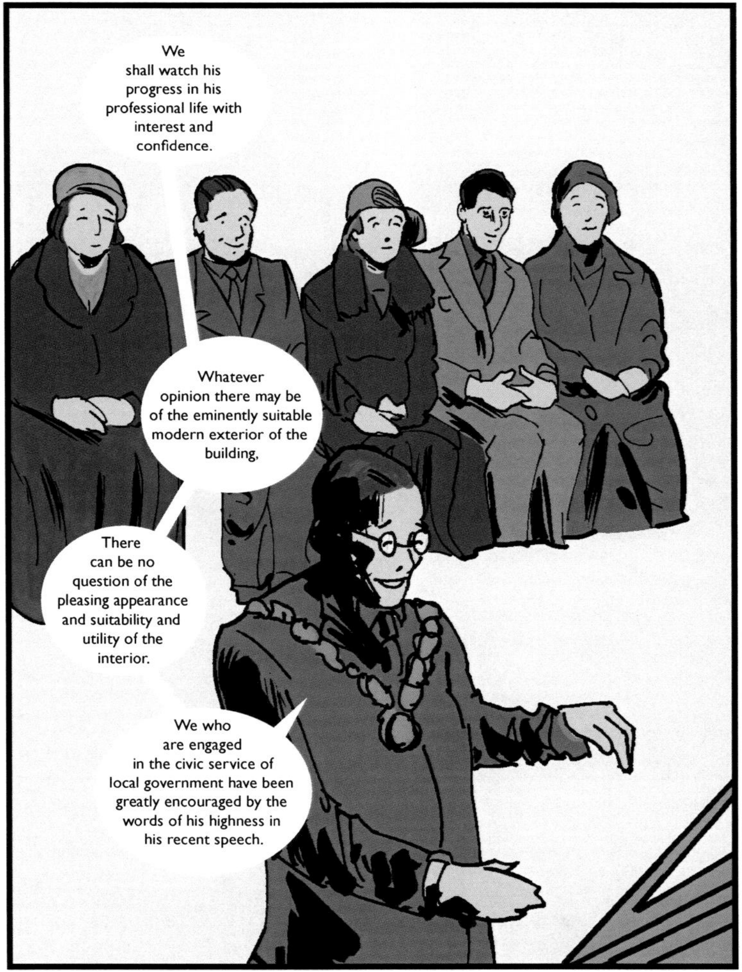
We shall watch his progress in his professional life with interest and confidence.
Whatever opinion there may be of the eminently suitable modern exterior of the building,
There can be no question of the pleasing appearance and suitability and utility of the interior.
We who are engaged in the civic service of local government have been greatly encouraged by the words of his highness in his recent speech.

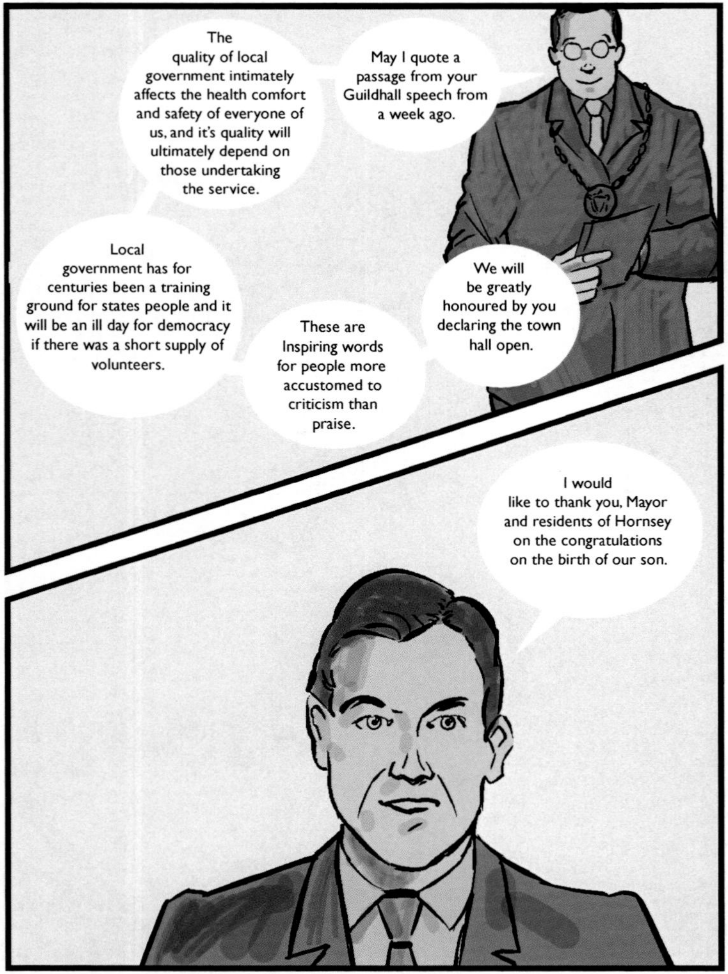
May I quote a passage from your Guildhall speech from a week ago.
The quality of local government intimately affects the health comfort and safety of everyone of us, and it's quality will ultimately depend on those undertaking the service.
Local government has for centuries been a training ground for states people and it will be an ill day for democracy if there was a short supply of volunteers.
These are Inspiring words for people more accustomed to criticism than praise.
We will be greatly honoured by you declaring the town hall open.
I would like to thank you, Mayor and residents of Hornsey on the congratulations on the birth of our son.

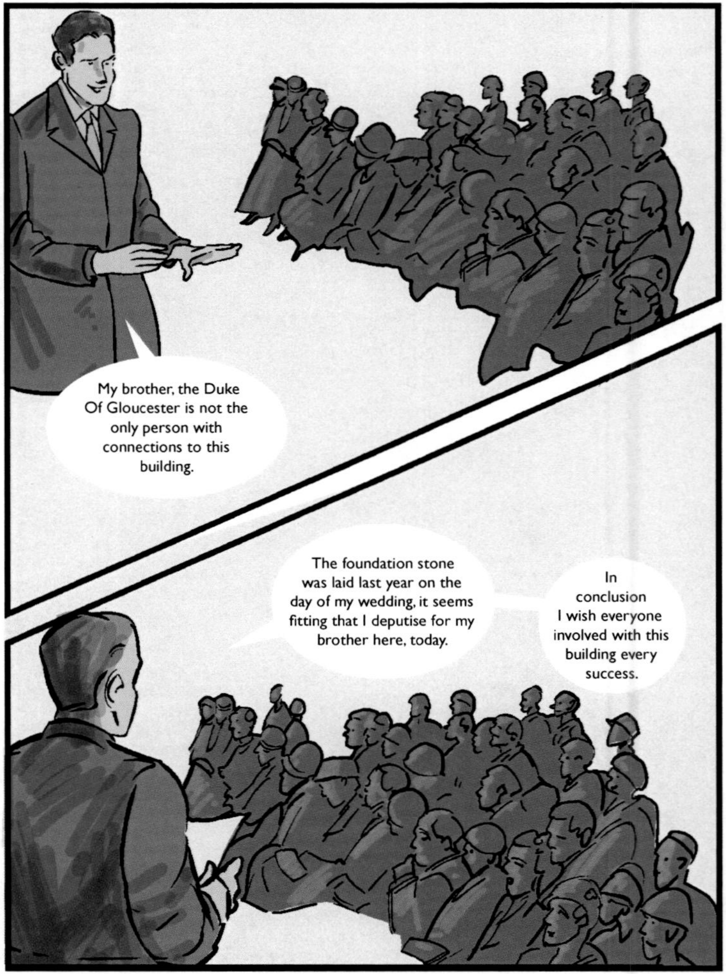
My brother, the Duke Of Gloucester is not the only person with connections to this building.
The foundation stone was laid last year on the day of my wedding, it seems fitting that I deputise for my brother here, today.
In conclusion I wish everyone involved with this building every success.

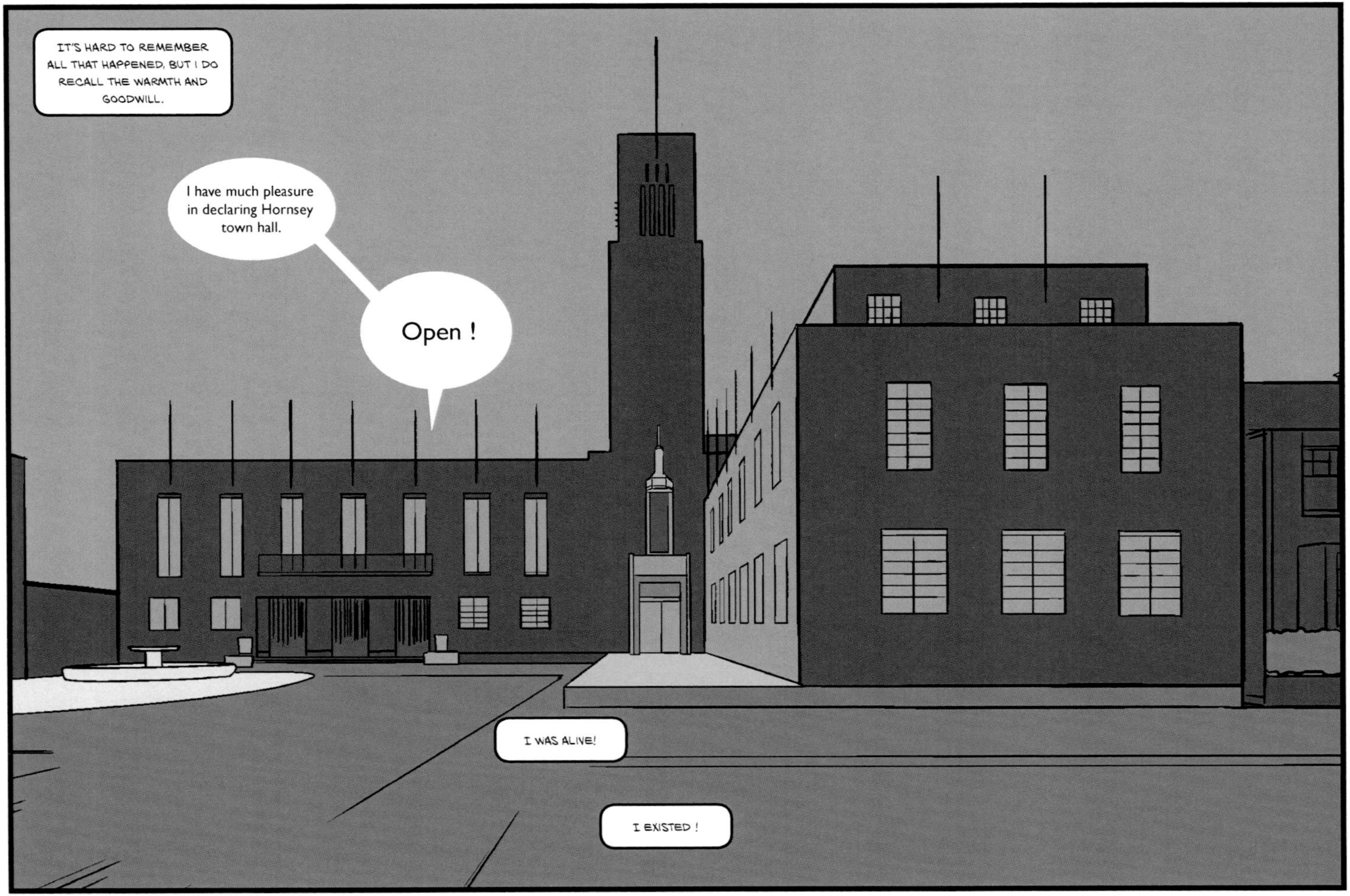
IT'S HARD TO REMEMBER ALL THAT HAPPENED, BUT I DO RECALL THE WARMTH AND GOODWILL.
I have much pleasure in declaring Hornsey town hall.
Open !
I WAS ALIVE!
I EXISTED !

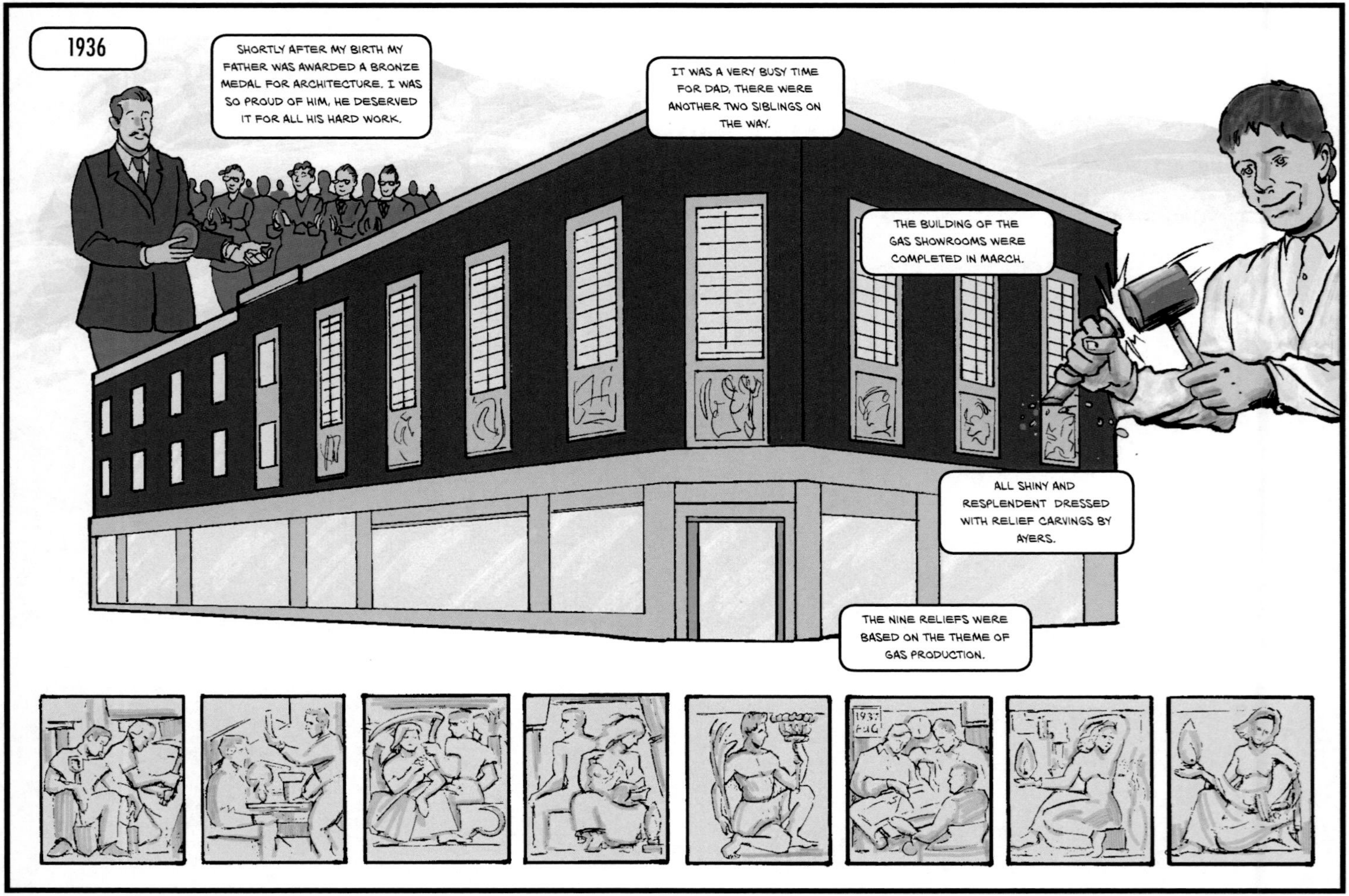
1936
SHORTLY AFTER MY BIRTH MY FATHER WAS AWARDED A BRONZE MEDAL FOR ARCHITECTURE. I WAS SO PROUD OF HIM, HE DESERVED IT FOR ALL HIS HARD WORK.
IT WAS A VERY BUSY TIME FOR DAD, THERE WERE ANOTHER TWO SIBLINGS ON THE WAY.
THE BUILDING OF THE GAS SHOWROOMS WERE COMPLETED IN MARCH.
ALL SHINY AND RESPLENDENT DRESSED WITH RELIEF CARVINGS BY AYERS.
THE NINE RELIEFS WERE BASED ON THE THEME OF GAS PRODUCTION.

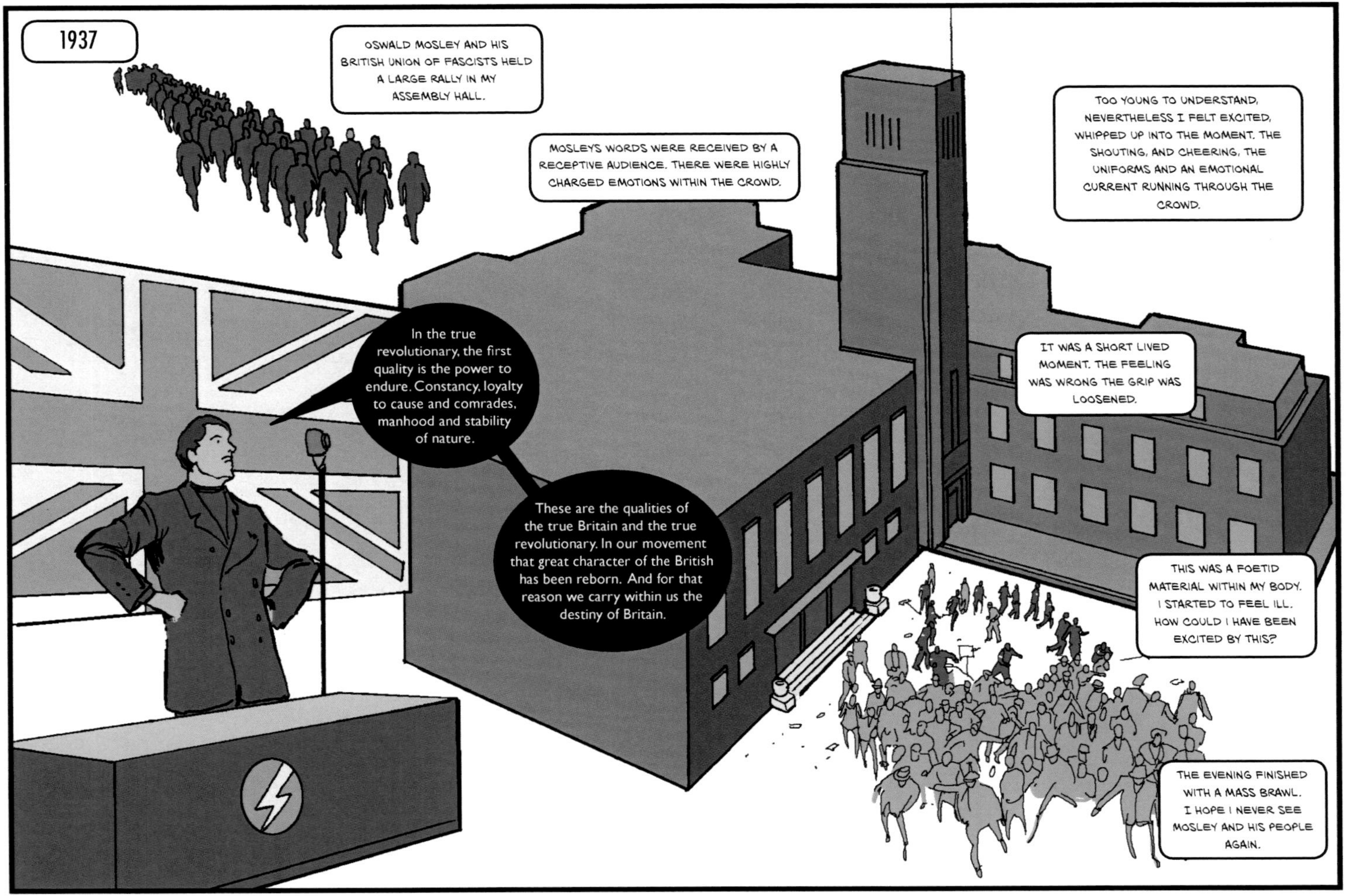
1937
OSWALD MOSLEY AND HIS BRITISH UNION OF FASCISTS HELD A LARGE RALLY IN MY ASSEMBLY HALL.
MOSLEYS WORDS WERE RECEIVED BY A RECEPTIVE AUDIENCE. THERE WERE HIGHLY CHARGED EMOTIONS WITHIN THE CROWD.
TOO YOUNG TO UNDERSTAND, NEVERTHELESS I FELT EXCITED, WHIPPED UP INTO THE MOMENT. THE SHOUTING, AND CHEERING, THE UNIFORMS AND AN EMOTIONAL CURRENT RUNNING THROUGH THE CROWD.
In the true revolutionary, the first quality is the power to endure. Constancy, loyalty to cause and comrades, manhood and stability of nature.
These are the qualities of the true Britain and the true revolutionary. In our movement that great character of the British has been reborn. And for that reason we carry within us the destiny of Britain.
IT WAS A SHORT LIVED MOMENT. THE FEELING WAS WRONG THE GRIP WAS LOOSENED.
THIS WAS A FOETID MATERIAL WITHIN MY BODY. I STARTED TO FEEL ILL. HOW COULD I HAVE BEEN EXCITED BY THIS?
THE EVENING FINISHED WITH A MASS BRAWL. I HOPE I NEVER SEE MOSLEY AND HIS PEOPLE AGAIN.

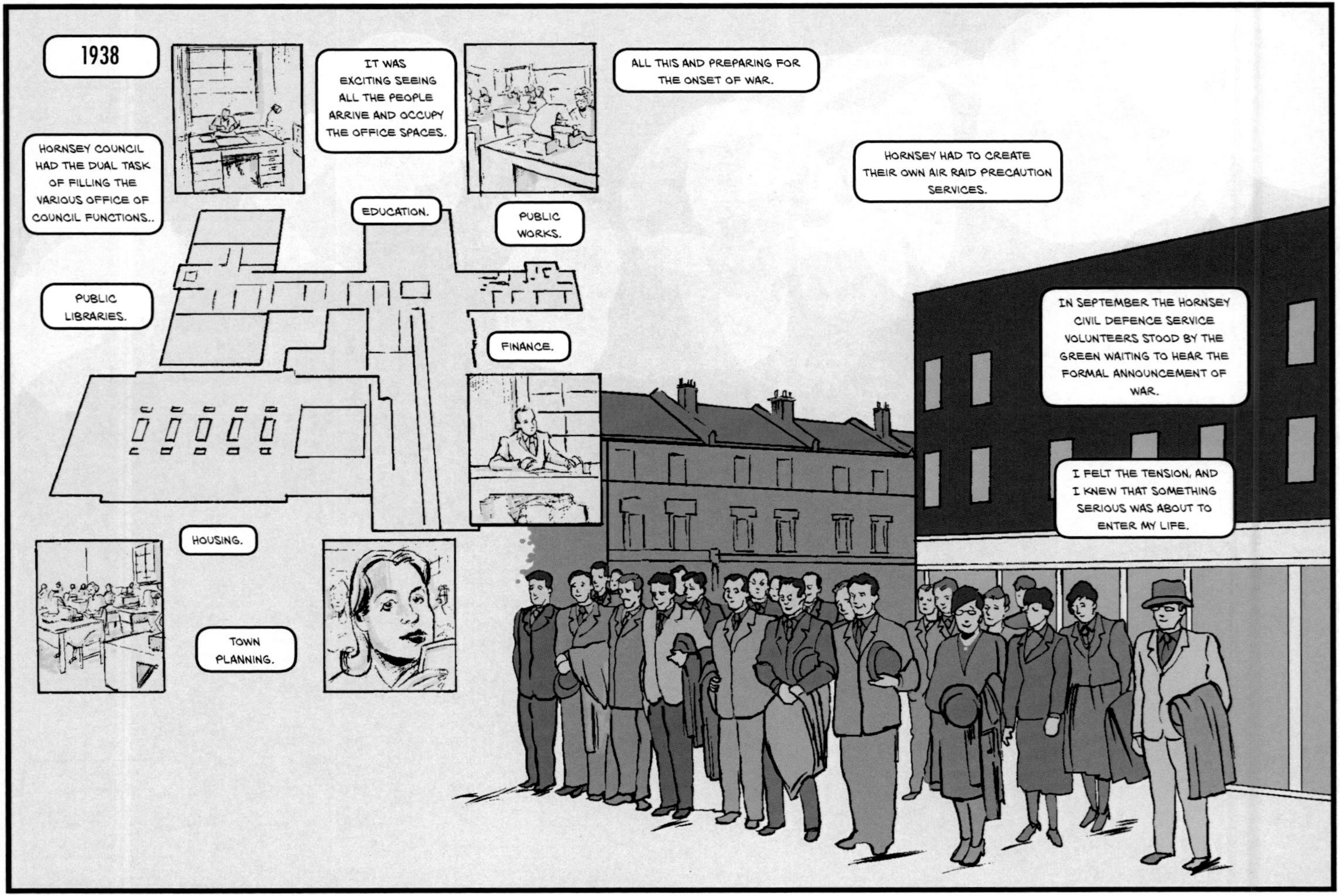
1938
HORNSEY COUNCIL HAD THE DUAL TASK OF FILLING THE VARIOUS OFFICE OF COUNCIL FUNCTIONS..
IT WAS EXCITING SEEING ALL THE PEOPLE ARRIVE AND OCCUPY THE OFFICE SPACES.
ALL THIS AND PREPARING FOR THE ONSET OF WAR.
EDUCATION.
PUBLIC WORKS.
PUBLIC LIBRARIES.
FINANCE.
HOUSING.
TOWN PLANNING.
HORNSEY HAD TO CREATE THEIR OWN AIR RAID PRECAUTION SERVICES.
IN SEPTEMBER THE HORNSEY CIVIL DEFENCE SERVICE VOLUNTEERS STOOD BY THE GREEN WAITING TO HEAR THE FORMAL ANNOUNCEMENT OF WAR.
I FELT THE TENSION, AND I KNEW THAT SOMETHING SERIOUS WAS ABOUT TO ENTER MY LIFE.

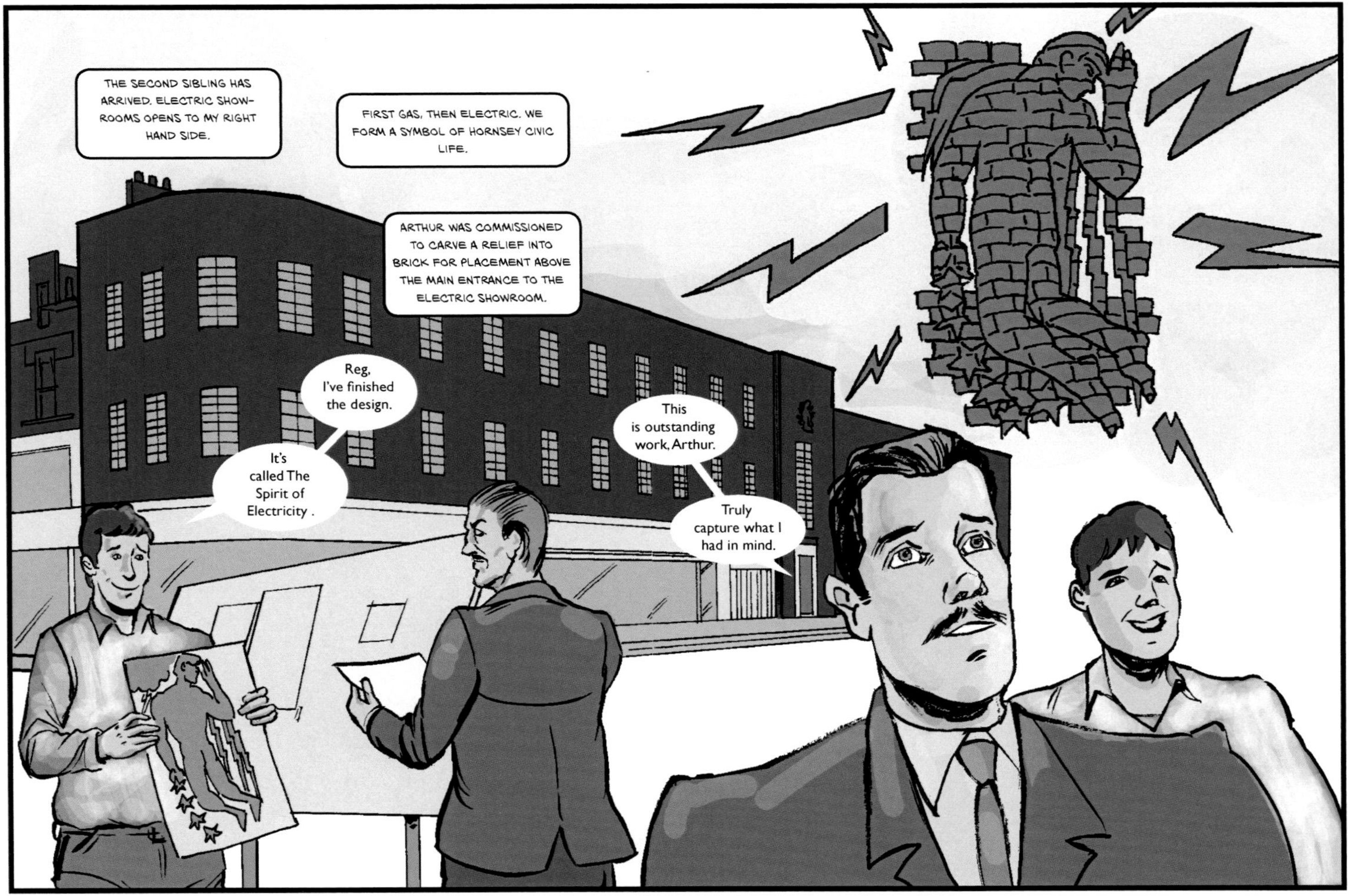
THE SECOND SIBLING HAS ARRIVED. ELECTRIC SHOW-ROOMS OPENS TO MY RIGHT HAND SIDE.
FIRST GAS, THEN ELECTRIC. WE FORM A SYMBOL OF HORNSEY CIVIC LIFE.
ARTHUR WAS COMMISSIONED TO CARVE A RELIEF INTO BRICK FOR PLACEMENT ABOVE THE MAIN ENTRANCE TO THE ELECTRIC SHOWROOM.
Reg, I've finished the design.
It's called The Spirit of Electricity .
This is outstanding work, Arthur.
Truly capture what I had in mind.

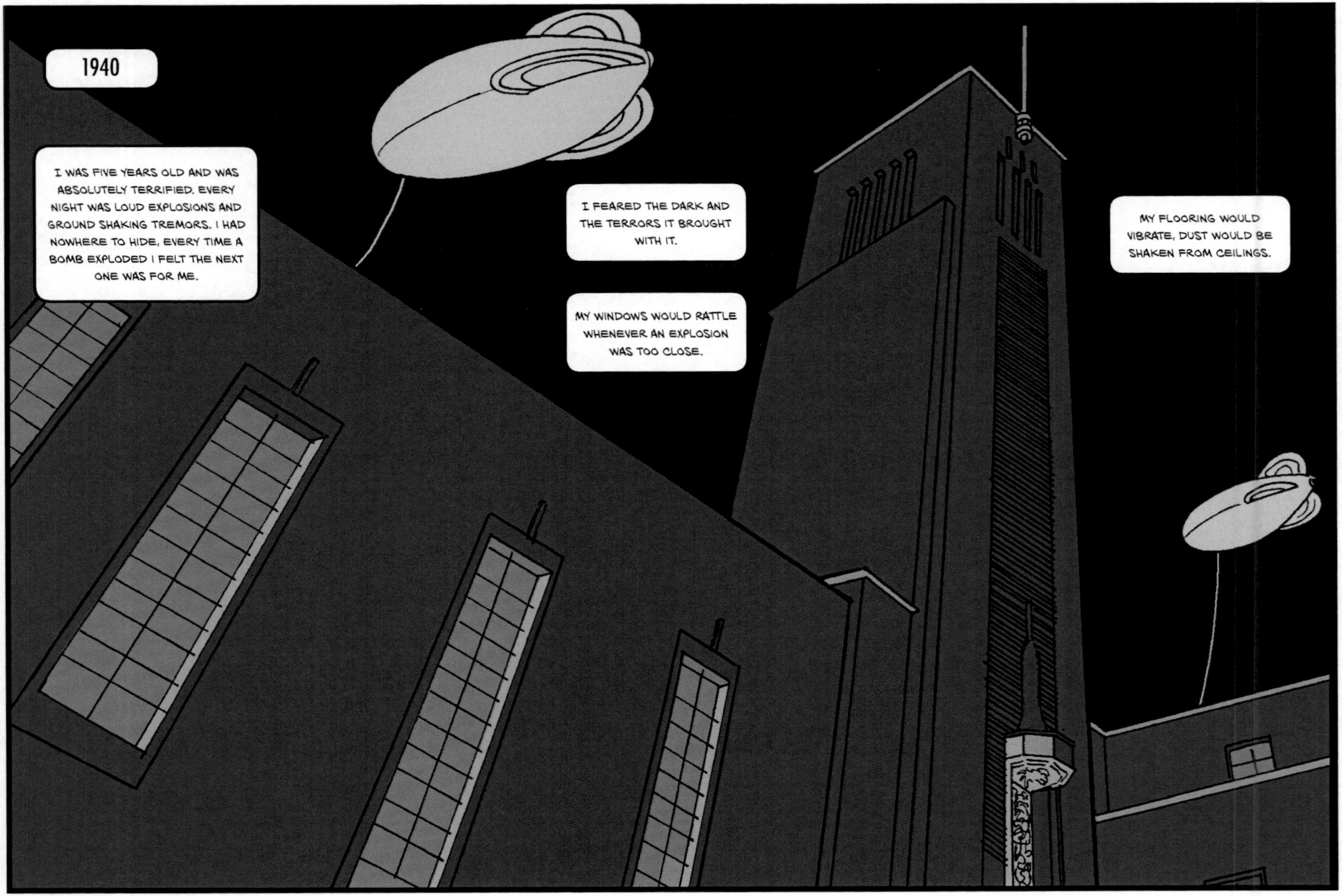
1940
I WAS FIVE YEARS OLD AND WAS ABSOLUTELY TERRIFIED. EVERY NIGHT WAS LOUD EXPLOSIONS AND GROUND SHAKING TREMORS. I HAD NOWHERE TO HIDE, EVERY TIME A BOMB EXPLODED I FELT THE NEXT ONE WAS FOR ME.
I FEARED THE DARK AND THE TERRORS IT BROUGHT WITH IT.
MY WINDOWS WOULD RATTLE WHENEVER AN EXPLOSION WAS TOO CLOSE.
MY FLOORING WOULD VIBRATE, DUST WOULD BE SHAKEN FROM CEILINGS.

BOMBERS WOULD DRONE OVERHEAD, NIGHT AFTER NIGHT.
IT'S MY TURN NEXT.
THIS IS WHAT I KEPT THINKING, OVER AND OVER.
1942
I WAS ON MY OWN. I WAS SO FRIGHTENED.
I DIDN'T UNDERSTAND WHAT WAS HAPPENING.
I JUST WANTED IT TO STOP.
DUKE OF KENT DIES.
LEFT ON THE RECEPTION DESK, A NEWSPAPER HAS BROUGHT ME TERRIBLY SAD NEWS.
AFTER GRACING MY ASSEMBLY HALL WITH HIS FINE SPEECH AND KIND WORDS.
HE IS NO LONGER WITH US.
HE WILL ALWAYS BE A VOICE IN THIS ROOM, THOUGH.
I WILL NEVER FORGET.

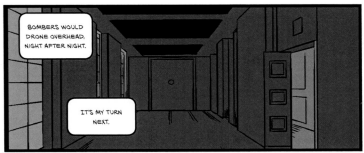

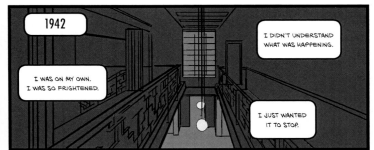

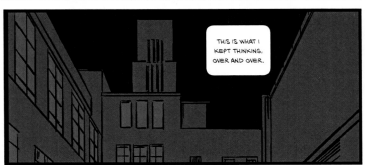

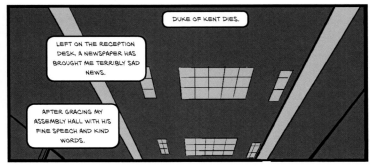

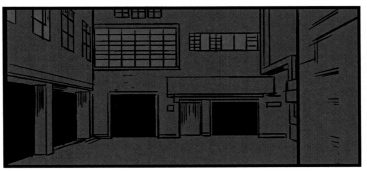

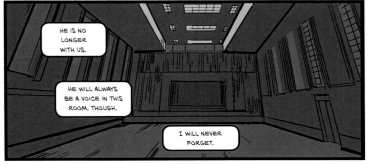

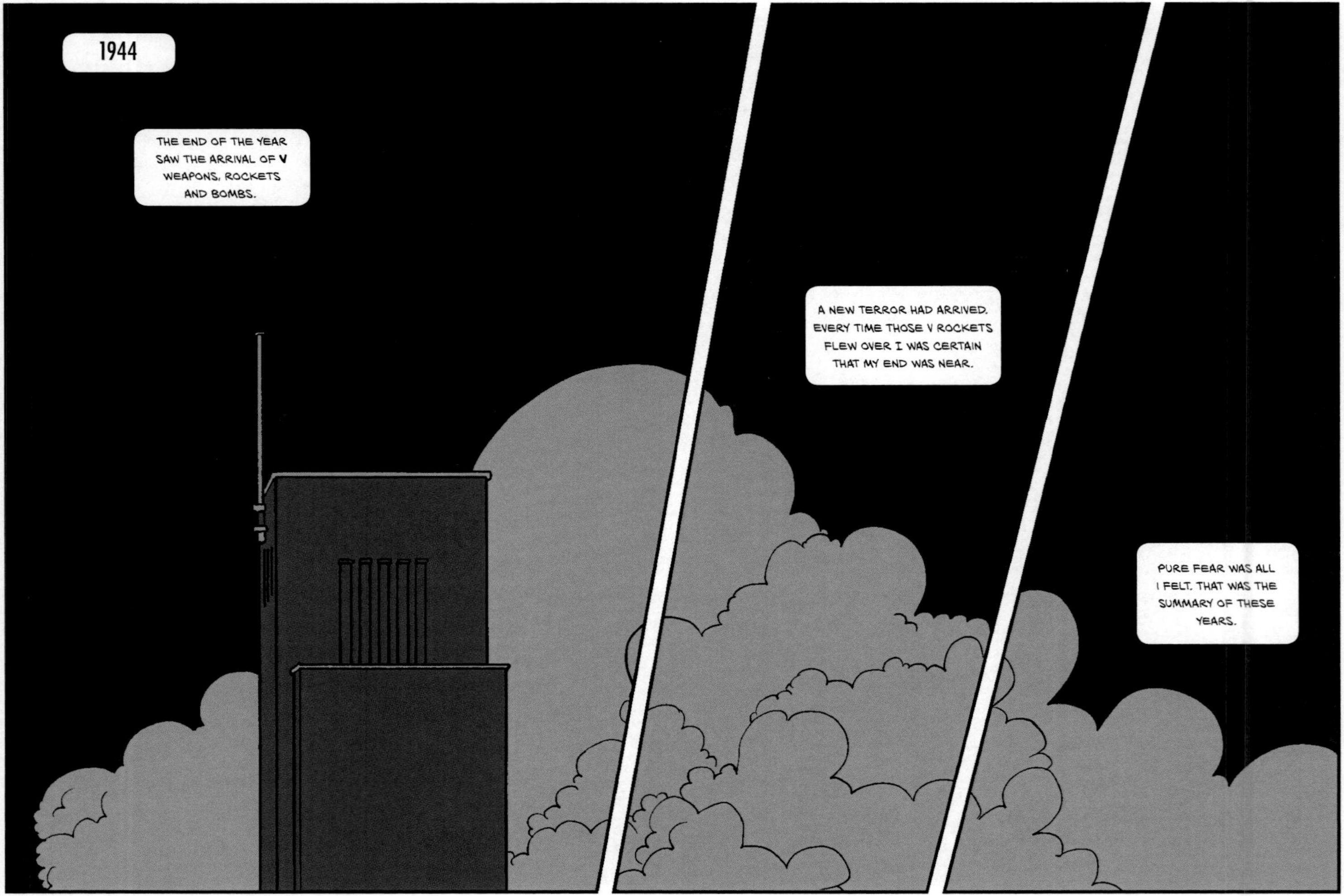
1944
THE END OF THE YEAR SAW THE ARRIVAL OF V WEAPONS, ROCKETS AND BOMBS.
A NEW TERROR HAD ARRIVED. EVERY TIME THOSE V ROCKETS FLEW OVER I WAS CERTAIN THAT MY END WAS NEAR.
PURE FEAR WAS ALL I FELT. THAT WAS THE SUMMARY OF THESE YEARS.

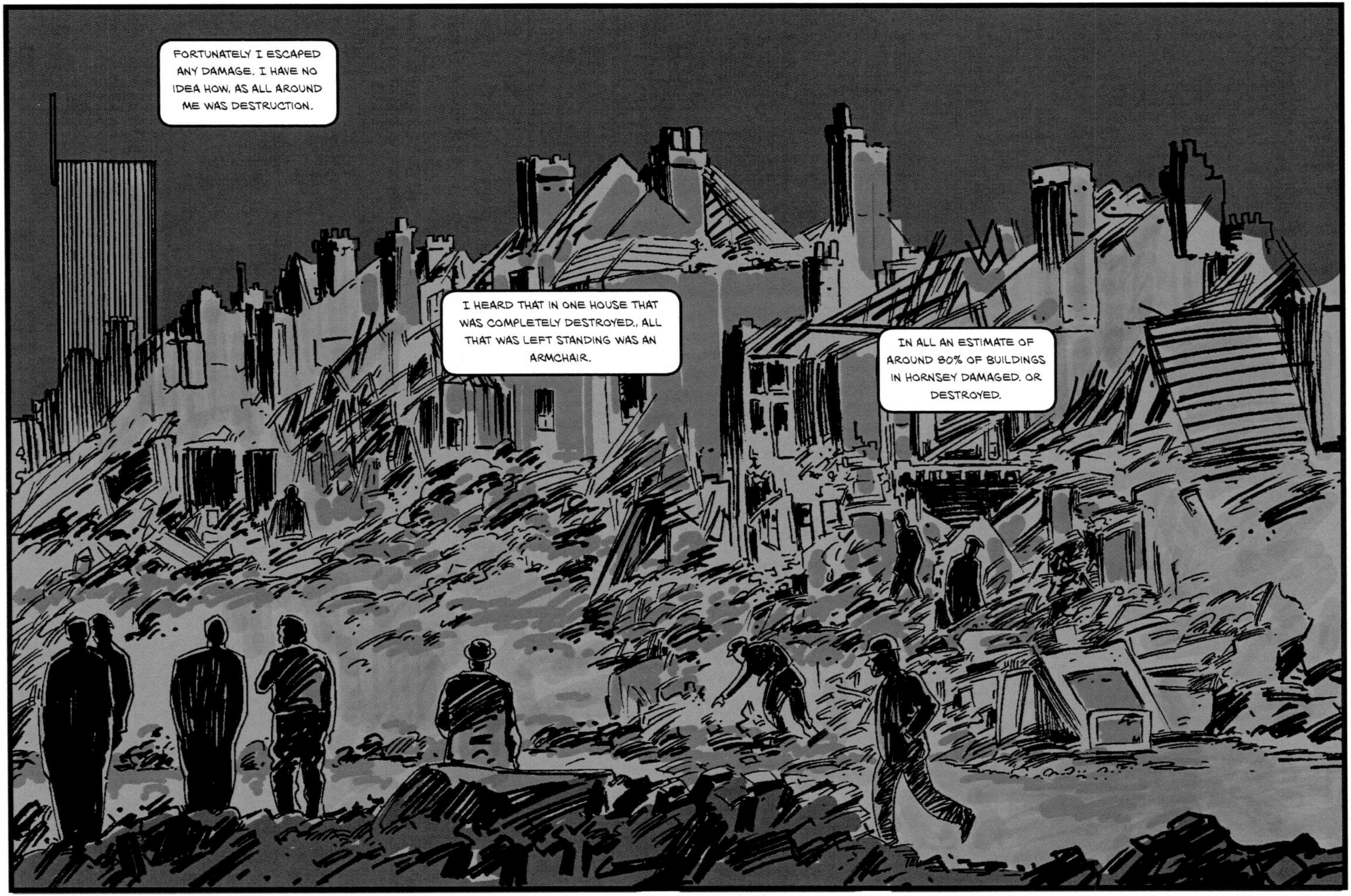
FORTUNATELY I ESCAPED ANY DAMAGE. I HAVE NO IDEA HOW, AS ALL AROUND ME WAS DESTRUCTION.
I HEARD THAT IN ONE HOUSE THAT WAS COMPLETELY DESTROYED., ALL THAT WAS LEFT STANDING WAS AN ARMCHAIR.
IN ALL AN ESTIMATE OF AROUND 80% OF BUILDINGS IN HORNSEY DAMAGED. OR DESTROYED.

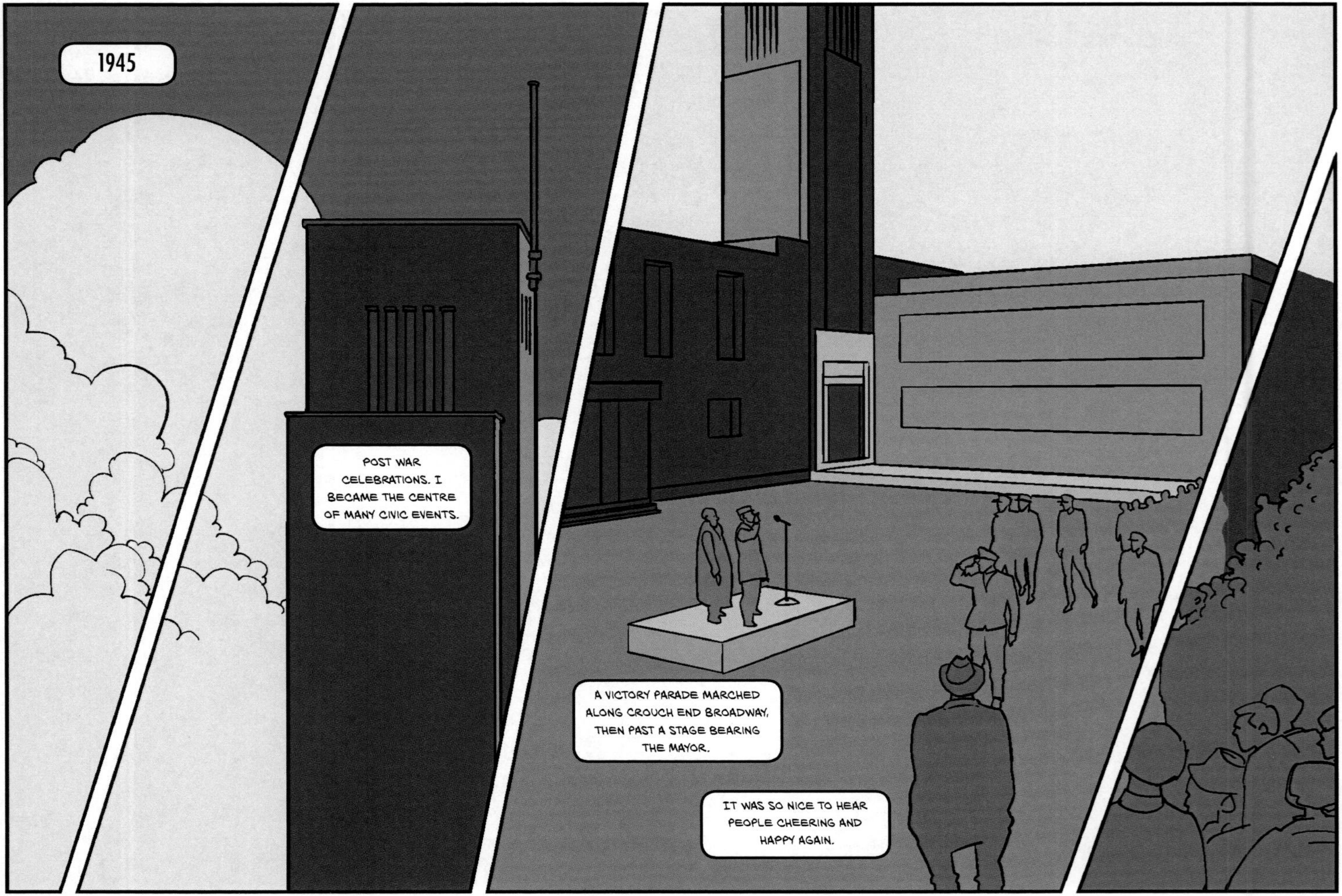
1945
POST WAR CELEBRATIONS. I BECAME THE CENTRE OF MANY CIVIC EVENTS.
A VICTORY PARADE MARCHED ALONG CROUCH END BROADWAY, THEN PAST A STAGE BEARING THE MAYOR.
IT WAS SO NICE TO HEAR PEOPLE CHEERING AND HAPPY AGAIN.

WAR PRISONER COURTS WERE HELD IN THE MAYORS CHAMBER.

A SUCCESSION OF GREY FACED DEFEATED PEOPLE ENTERED THE ROOM.

A HEAD BOWED OR A FACE WITH A BLANK STARE.

SENTENCES WERE PASSED FUTURES WERE DECIDED.

IT WAS A VERY SOMBRE PROCESS.

I WAS RELIEVED WHEN IT WAS COMPLETED.

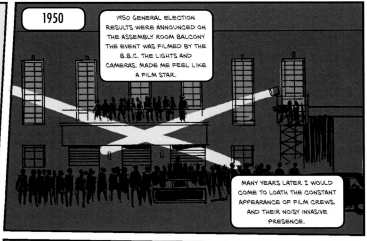

1950

1950 GENERAL ELECTION RESULTS WERE ANNOUNCED ON THE ASSEMBLY ROOM BALCONY THE EVENT WAS FILMED BY THE B.B.C. THE LIGHTS AND CAMERAS. MADE ME FEEL LIKE A FILM STAR.

MANY YEARS LATER I WOULD COME TO LOATH THE CONSTANT APPEARANCE OF FILM CREWS. AND THEIR NOISY INVASIVE PRESENCE.

1951

MY FLAG WAS FLOWN AT HALF MAST AS THE DEATH OF THE KING WAS ANNOUNCED TO THE NATION.

CHURCH BELLS RANG A MOURNFUL PEAL THROUGHOUT THE DAY.

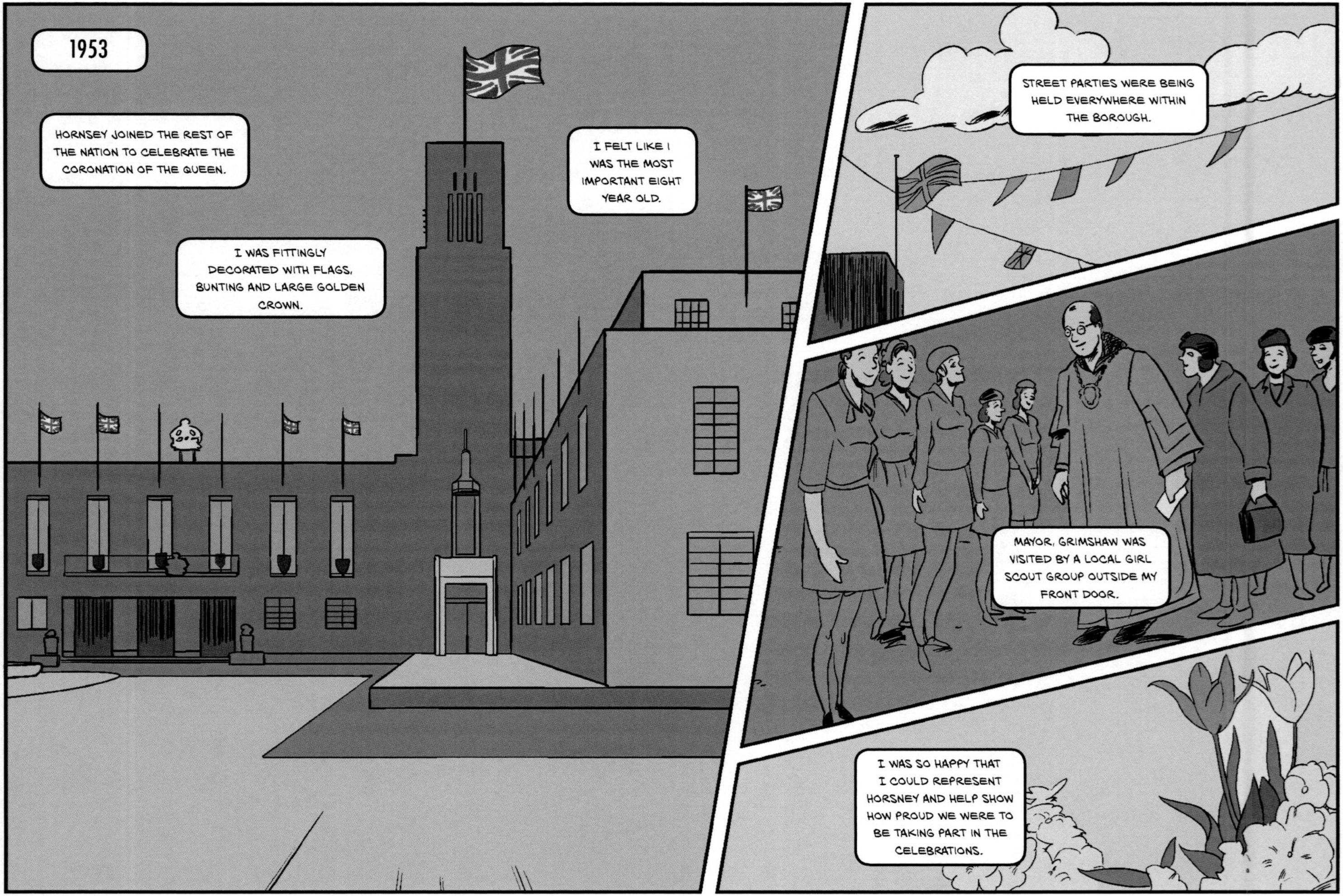
1953
HORNSEY JOINED THE REST OF THE NATION TO CELEBRATE THE CORONATION OF THE QUEEN.
I WAS FITTINGLY DECORATED WITH FLAGS, BUNTING AND LARGE GOLDEN CROWN.
I FELT LIKE I WAS THE MOST IMPORTANT EIGHT YEAR OLD.
STREET PARTIES WERE BEING HELD EVERYWHERE WITHIN THE BOROUGH.
MAYOR, GRIMSHAW WAS VISITED BY A LOCAL GIRL SCOUT GROUP OUTSIDE MY FRONT DOOR.
I WAS SO HAPPY THAT I COULD REPRESENT HORSNEY AND HELP SHOW HOW PROUD WE WERE TO BE TAKING PART IN THE CELEBRATIONS.

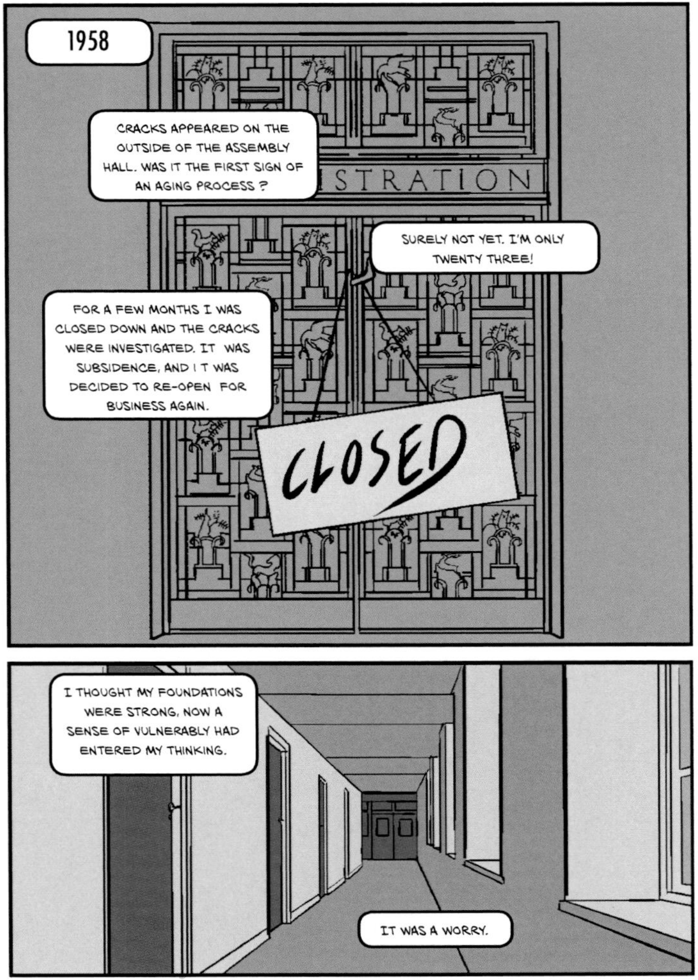
1958
CRACKS APPEARED ON THE OUTSIDE OF THE ASSEMBLY HALL. WAS IT THE FIRST SIGN OF AN AGING PROCESS ?
STRATION
SURELY NOT YET. I'M ONLY TWENTY THREE!
FOR A FEW MONTHS I WAS CLOSED DOWN AND THE CRACKS WERE INVESTIGATED. IT WAS SUBSIDENCE, AND I T WAS DECIDED TO RE-OPEN FOR BUSINESS AGAIN.
CLOSED
I THOUGHT MY FOUNDATIONS WERE STRONG, NOW A SENSE OF VULNERABLY HAD ENTERED MY THINKING.
IT WAS A WORRY.

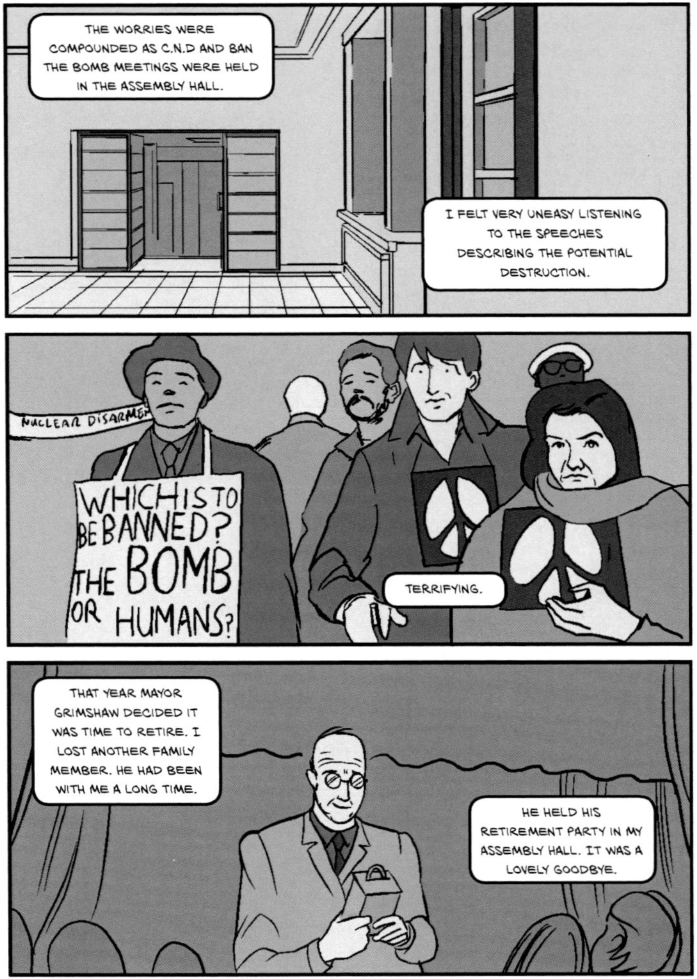
THE WORRIES WERE COMPOUNDED AS C.N.D AND BAN THE BOMB MEETINGS WERE HELD IN THE ASSEMBLY HALL.
I FELT VERY UNEASY LISTENING TO THE SPEECHES DESCRIBING THE POTENTIAL DESTRUCTION.
NUCLEAR DISARM
WHICH IS TO BE BANNED? THE BOMB OR HUMANS?
TERRIFYING.
THAT YEAR MAYOR GRIMSHAW DECIDED IT WAS TIME TO RETIRE. I LOST ANOTHER FAMILY MEMBER. HE HAD BEEN WITH ME A LONG TIME.
HE HELD HIS RETIREMENT PARTY IN MY ASSEMBLY HALL. IT WAS A LOVELY GOODBYE.

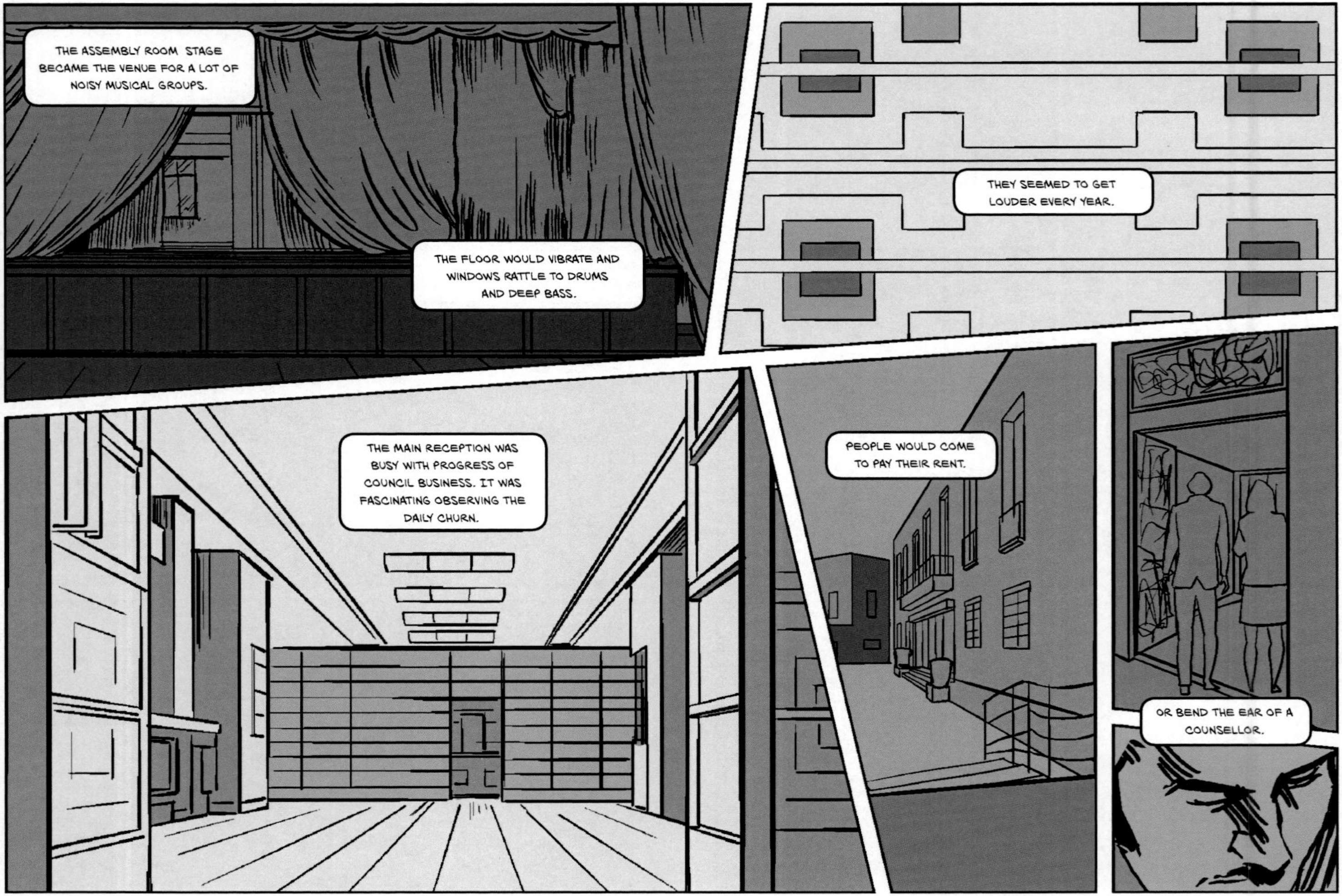
THE ASSEMBLY ROOM STAGE BECAME THE VENUE FOR A LOT OF NOISY MUSICAL GROUPS.
THE FLOOR WOULD VIBRATE AND WINDOWS RATTLE TO DRUMS AND DEEP BASS.
THEY SEEMED TO GET LOUDER EVERY YEAR.
THE MAIN RECEPTION WAS BUSY WITH PROGRESS OF COUNCIL BUSINESS. IT WAS FASCINATING OBSERVING THE DAILY CHURN.
PEOPLE WOULD COME TO PAY THEIR RENT.
OR BEND THE EAR OF A COUNSELLOR.

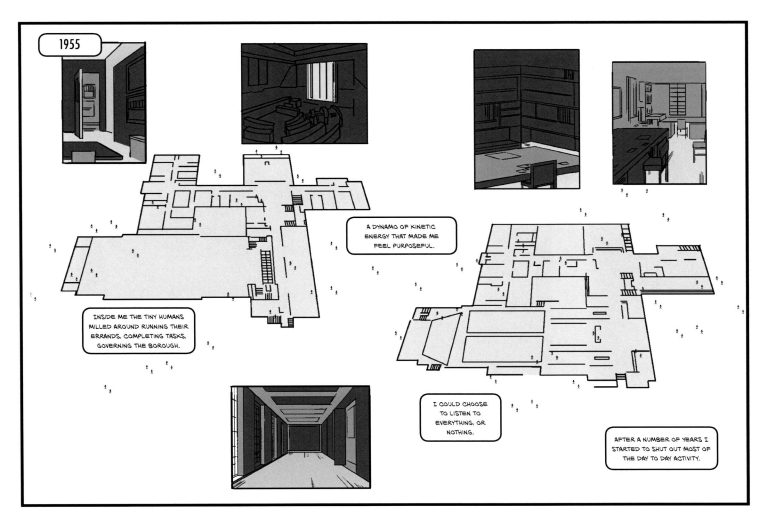

1955

A DYNAMO OF KINETIC ENERGY THAT MADE ME FEEL PURPOSEFUL.

INSIDE ME THE TINY HUMANS MILLED AROUND RUNNING THEIR ERRANDS, COMPLETING TASKS, GOVERNING THE BOROUGH.

I COULD CHOOSE TO LISTEN TO EVERYTHING, OR NOTHING.

AFTER A NUMBER OF YEARS I STARTED TO SHUT OUT MOST OF THE DAY TO DAY ACTIVITY.

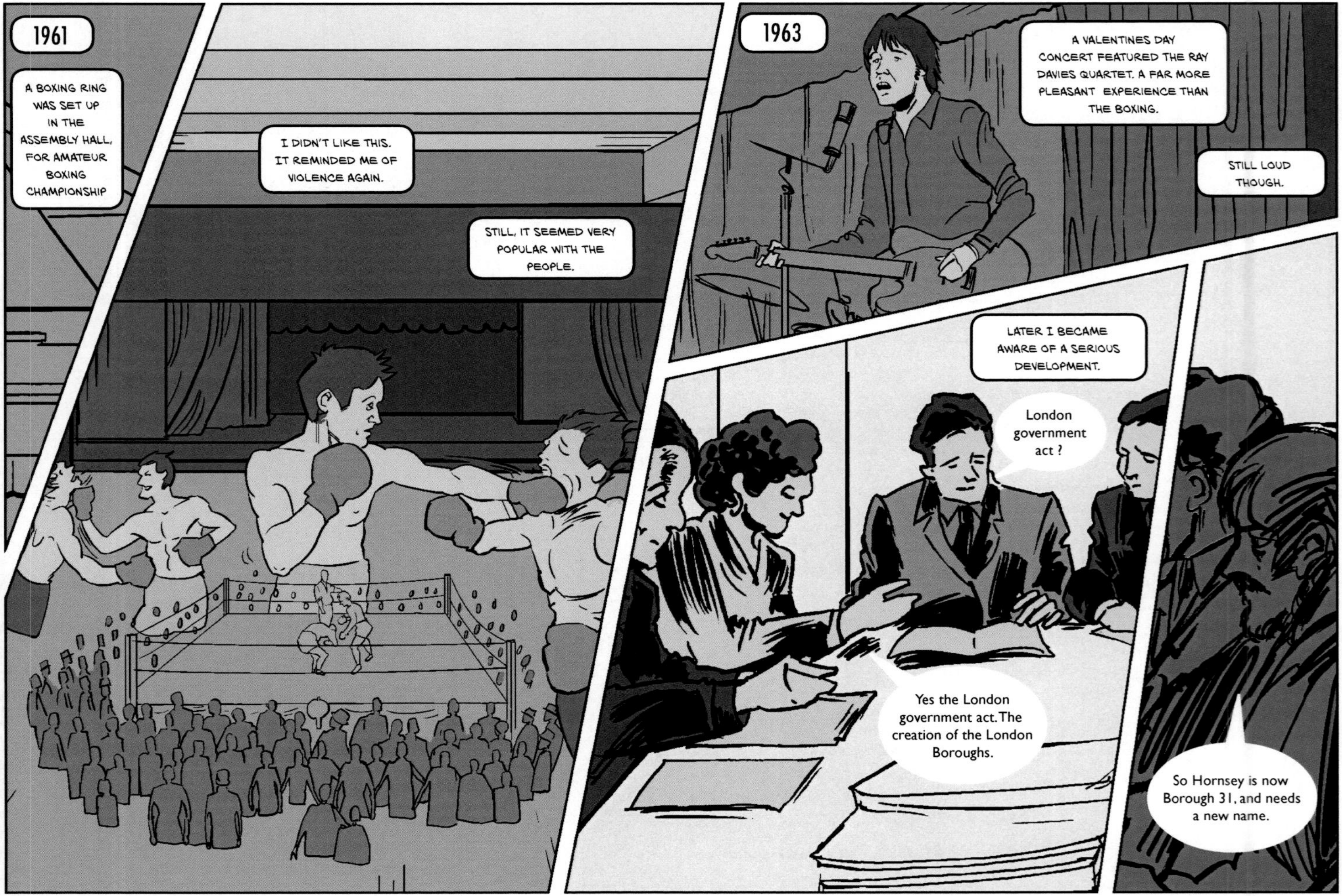

1961
A BOXING RING WAS SET UP IN THE ASSEMBLY HALL, FOR AMATEUR BOXING CHAMPIONSHIP
I DIDN'T LIKE THIS. IT REMINDED ME OF VIOLENCE AGAIN.
STILL, IT SEEMED VERY POPULAR WITH THE PEOPLE.
1963
A VALENTINES DAY CONCERT FEATURED THE RAY DAVIES QUARTET. A FAR MORE PLEASANT EXPERIENCE THAN THE BOXING.
STILL LOUD THOUGH.
LATER I BECAME AWARE OF A SERIOUS DEVELOPMENT.
London government act ?
Yes the London government act. The creation of the London Boroughs.
So Hornsey is now Borough 31, and needs a new name.

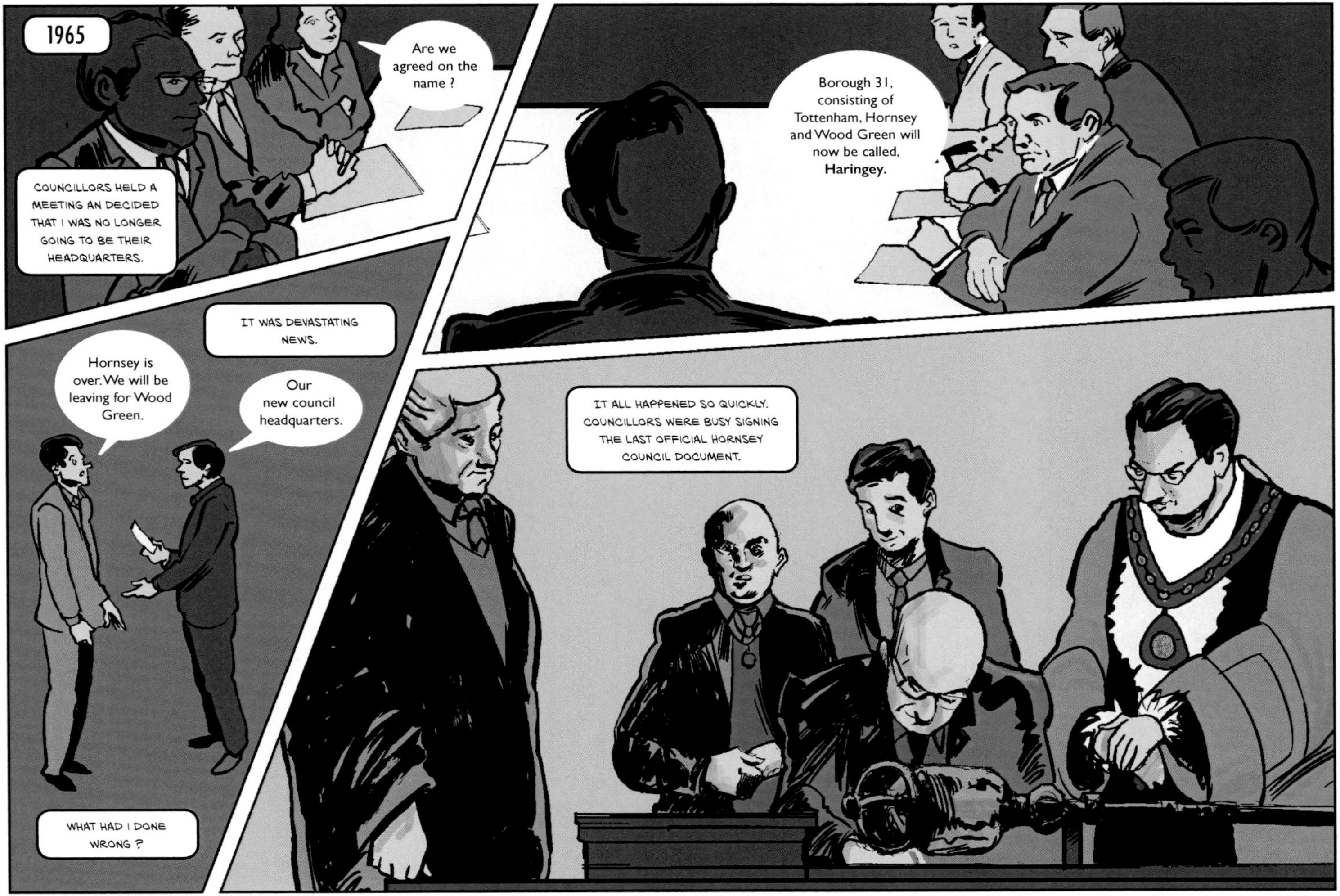
1965
Are we agreed on the name ?
COUNCILLORS HELD A MEETING AN DECIDED THAT I WAS NO LONGER GOING TO BE THEIR HEADQUARTERS.
Borough 31, consisting of Tottenham, Hornsey and Wood Green will now be called, **Haringey.**
IT WAS DEVASTATING NEWS.
Hornsey is over. We will be leaving for Wood Green.
Our new council headquarters.
WHAT HAD I DONE WRONG ?
IT ALL HAPPENED SO QUICKLY. COUNCILLORS WERE BUSY SIGNING THE LAST OFFICIAL HORNSEY COUNCIL DOCUMENT.

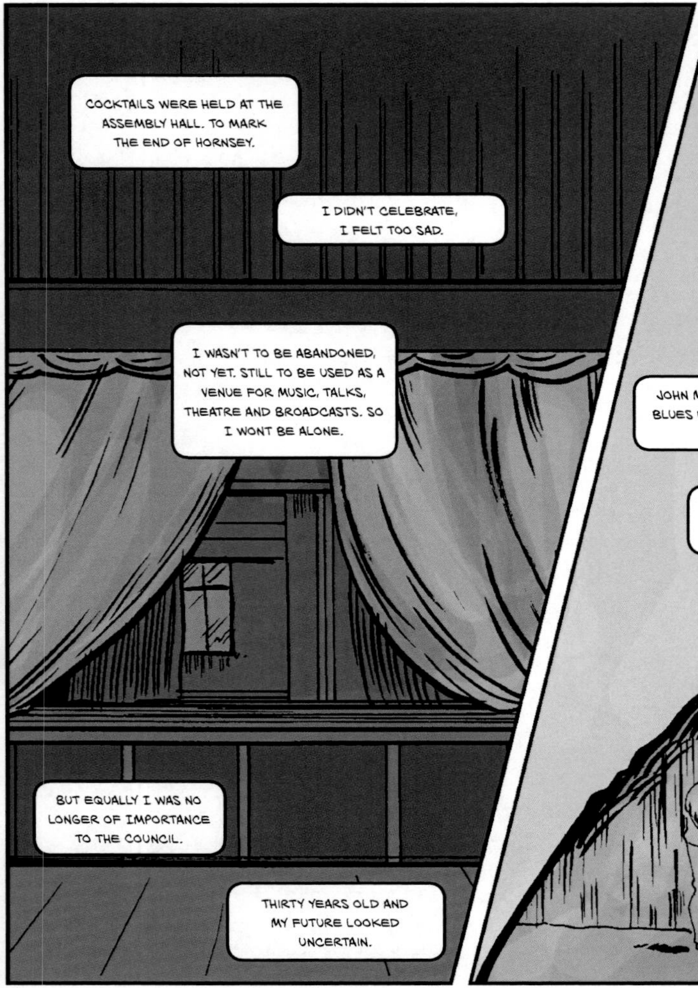
COCKTAILS WERE HELD AT THE ASSEMBLY HALL. TO MARK THE END OF HORNSEY.
I DIDN'T CELEBRATE, I FELT TOO SAD.
I WASN'T TO BE ABANDONED, NOT YET. STILL TO BE USED AS A VENUE FOR MUSIC, TALKS, THEATRE AND BROADCASTS. SO I WONT BE ALONE.
BUT EQUALLY I WAS NO LONGER OF IMPORTANCE TO THE COUNCIL.
THIRTY YEARS OLD AND MY FUTURE LOOKED UNCERTAIN.

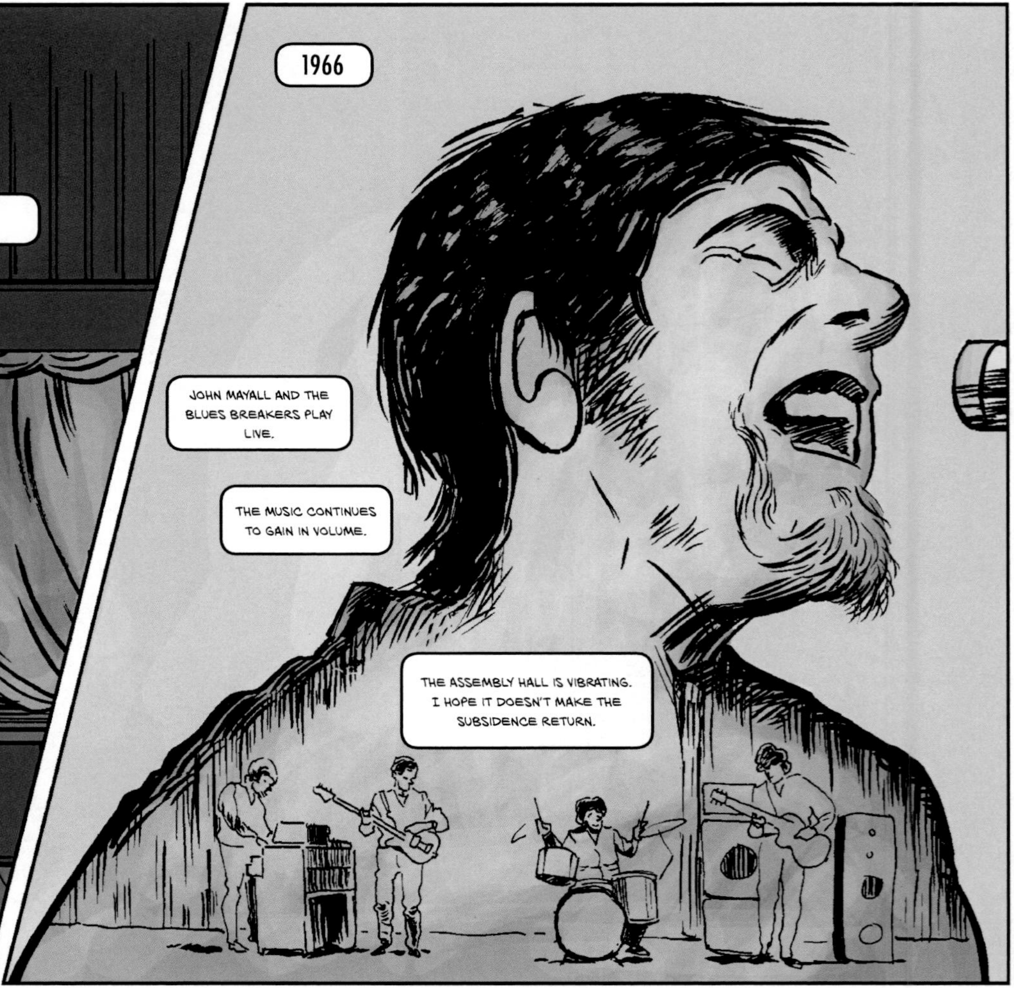
1966
JOHN MAYALL AND THE BLUES BREAKERS PLAY LIVE.
THE MUSIC CONTINUES TO GAIN IN VOLUME.
THE ASSEMBLY HALL IS VIBRATING. I HOPE IT DOESN'T MAKE THE SUBSIDENCE RETURN.

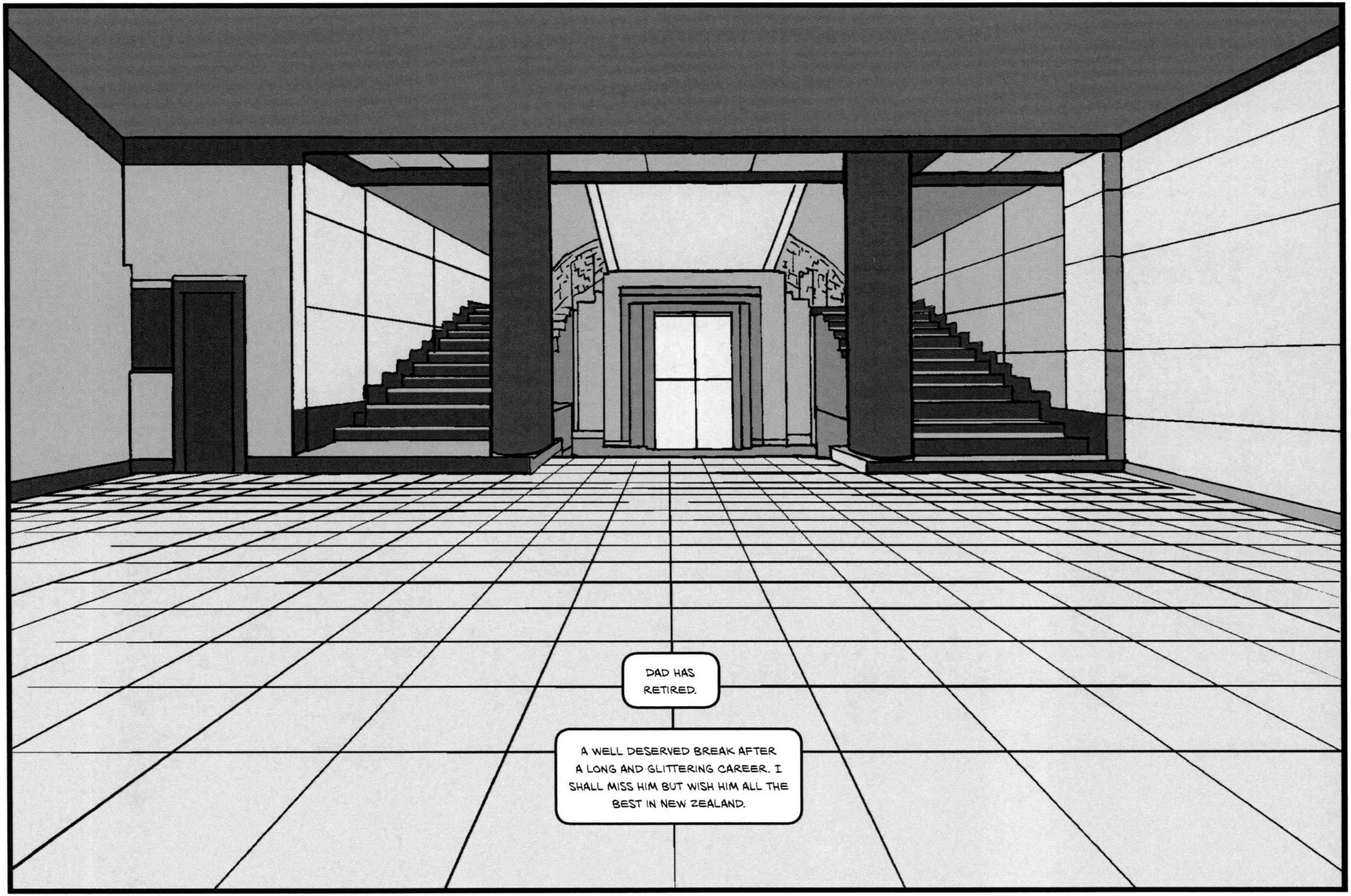
DAD HAS RETIRED.
A WELL DESERVED BREAK AFTER A LONG AND GLITTERING CAREER. I SHALL MISS HIM BUT WISH HIM ALL THE BEST IN NEW ZEALAND.

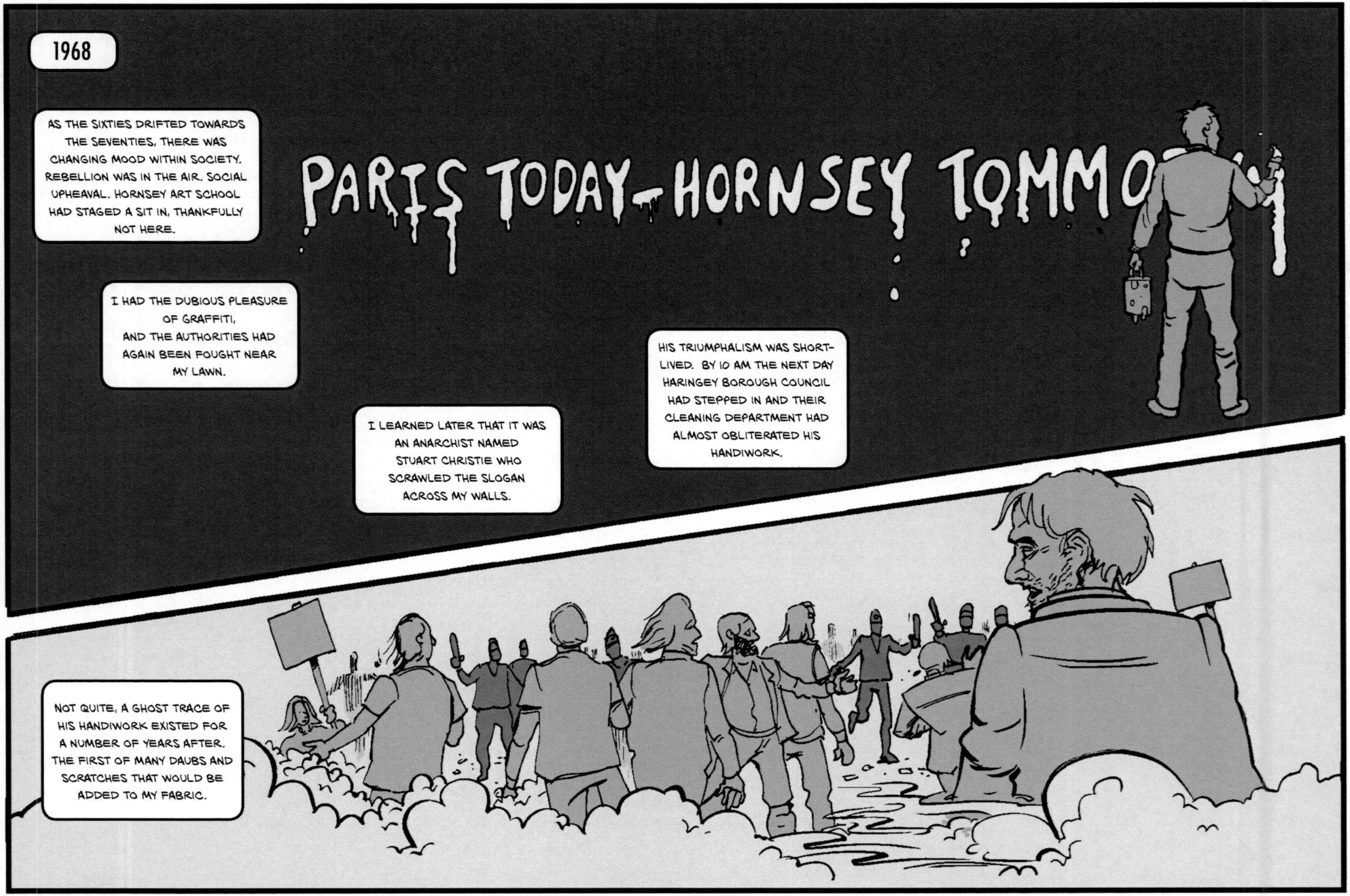

1968
AS THE SIXTIES DRIFTED TOWARDS THE SEVENTIES, THERE WAS CHANGING MOOD WITHIN SOCIETY. REBELLION WAS IN THE AIR. SOCIAL UPHEAVAL. HORNSEY ART SCHOOL HAD STAGED A SIT IN, THANKFULLY NOT HERE.
PARIS TODAY - HORNSEY TOMMO
I HAD THE DUBIOUS PLEASURE OF GRAFFITI, AND THE AUTHORITIES HAD AGAIN BEEN FOUGHT NEAR MY LAWN.
I LEARNED LATER THAT IT WAS AN ANARCHIST NAMED STUART CHRISTIE WHO SCRAWLED THE SLOGAN ACROSS MY WALLS.
HIS TRIUMPHALISM WAS SHORT-LIVED. BY 10 AM THE NEXT DAY HARINGEY BOROUGH COUNCIL HAD STEPPED IN AND THEIR CLEANING DEPARTMENT HAD ALMOST OBLITERATED HIS HANDIWORK.
NOT QUITE, A GHOST TRACE OF HIS HANDIWORK EXISTED FOR A NUMBER OF YEARS AFTER. THE FIRST OF MANY DAUBS AND SCRATCHES THAT WOULD BE ADDED TO MY FABRIC.

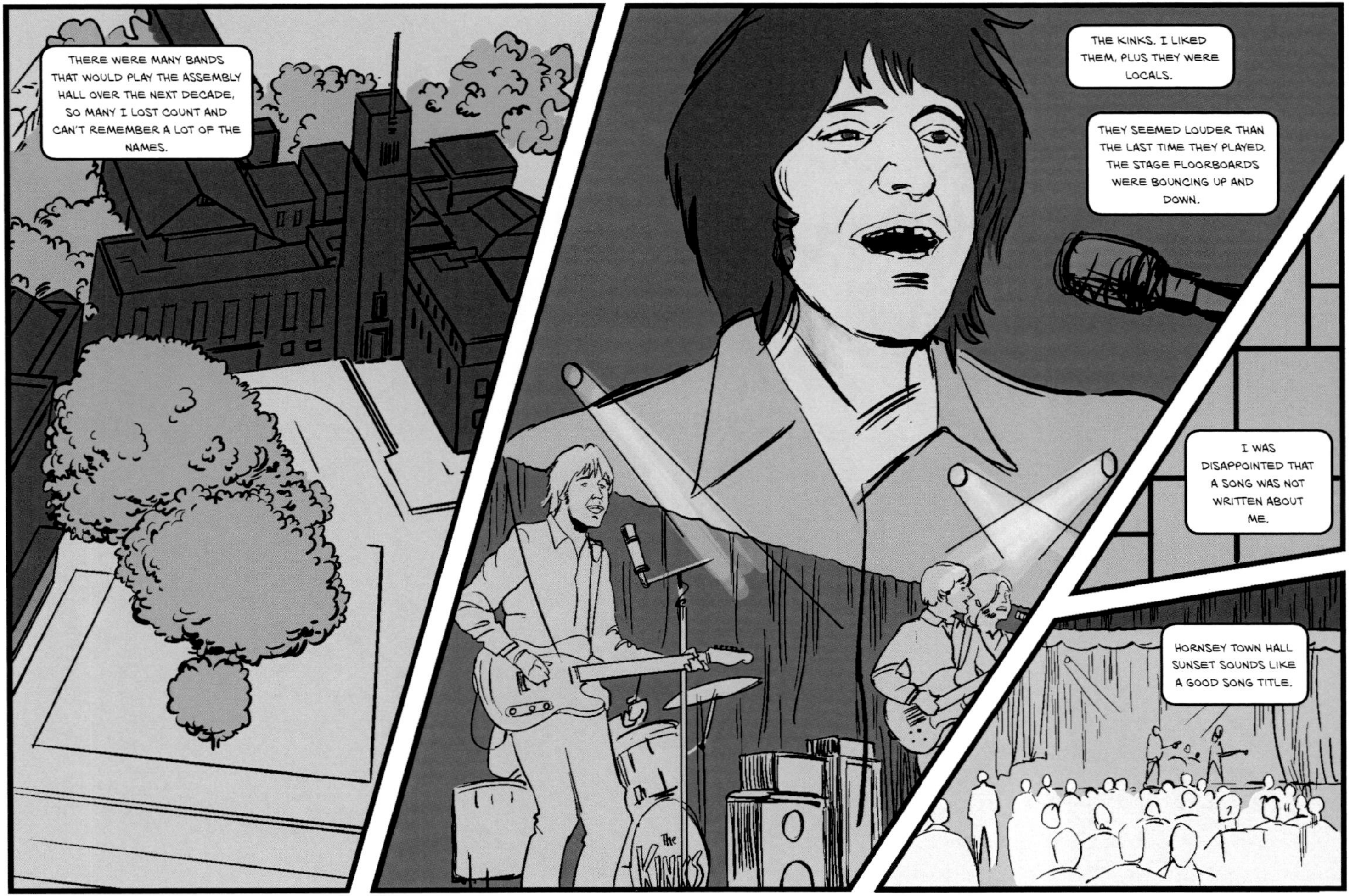

THERE WERE MANY BANDS THAT WOULD PLAY THE ASSEMBLY HALL OVER THE NEXT DECADE, SO MANY I LOST COUNT AND CAN'T REMEMBER A LOT OF THE NAMES.
THE KINKS. I LIKED THEM, PLUS THEY WERE LOCALS.
THEY SEEMED LOUDER THAN THE LAST TIME THEY PLAYED. THE STAGE FLOORBOARDS WERE BOUNCING UP AND DOWN.
The Kinks
I WAS DISAPPOINTED THAT A SONG WAS NOT WRITTEN ABOUT ME.
HORNSEY TOWN HALL SUNSET SOUNDS LIKE A GOOD SONG TITLE.

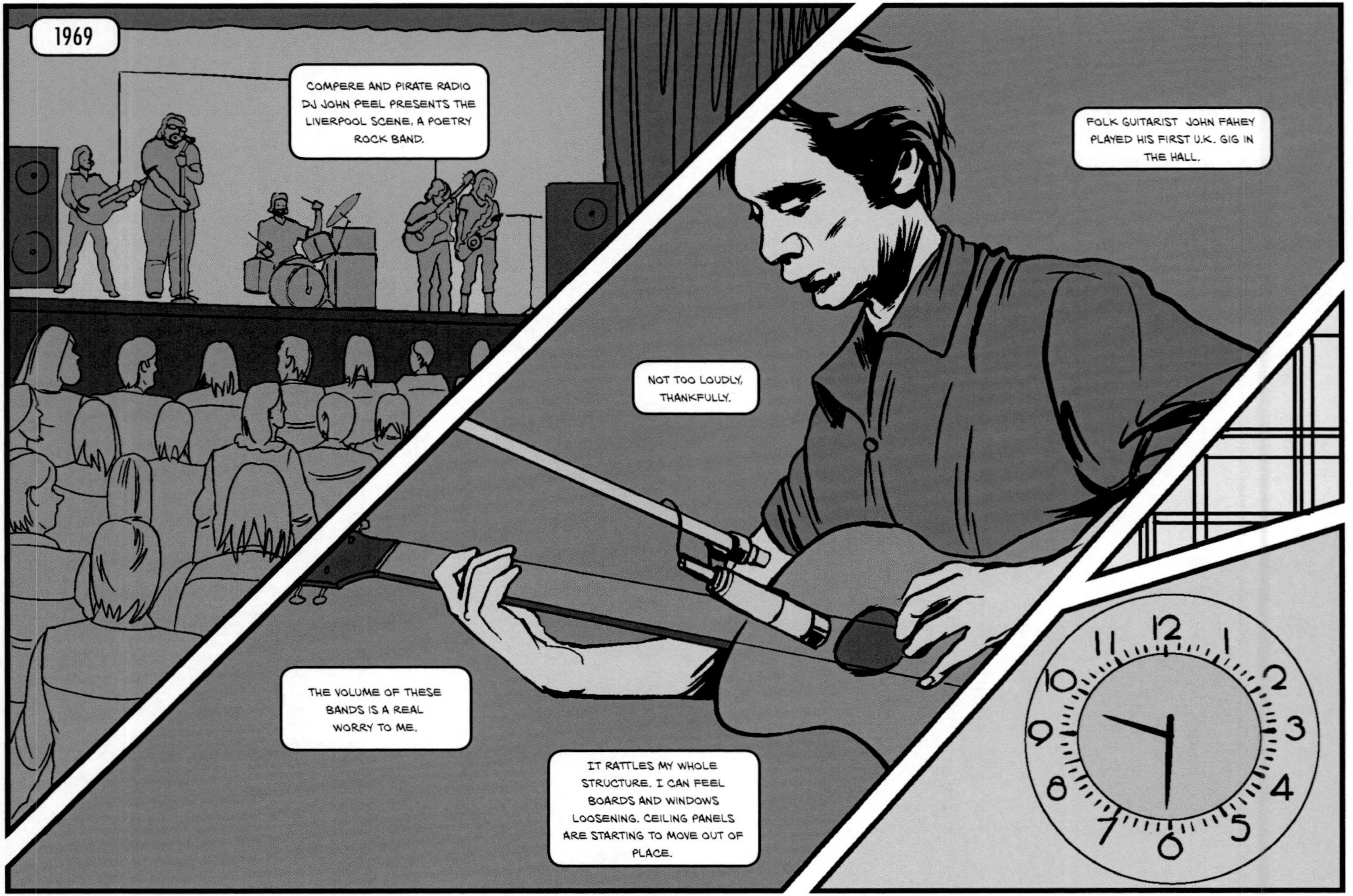
1969
COMPERE AND PIRATE RADIO DJ JOHN PEEL PRESENTS THE LIVERPOOL SCENE, A POETRY ROCK BAND.
FOLK GUITARIST JOHN FAHEY PLAYED HIS FIRST U.K. GIG IN THE HALL.
NOT TOO LOUDLY, THANKFULLY.
THE VOLUME OF THESE BANDS IS A REAL WORRY TO ME.
IT RATTLES MY WHOLE STRUCTURE. I CAN FEEL BOARDS AND WINDOWS LOOSENING. CEILING PANELS ARE STARTING TO MOVE OUT OF PLACE.
12
1
2
3
4
5
6
7
8
9
10
11

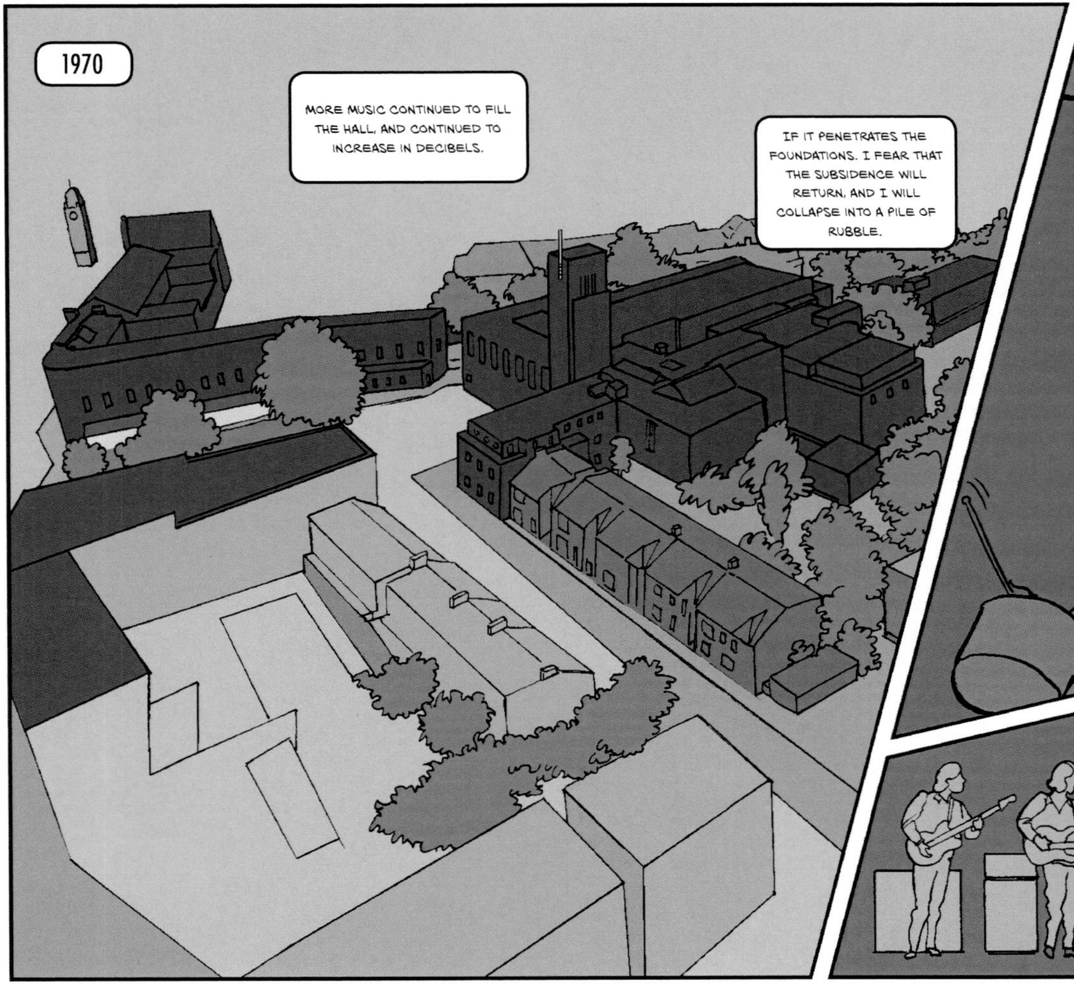
1970
MORE MUSIC CONTINUED TO FILL THE HALL, AND CONTINUED TO INCREASE IN DECIBELS.
IF IT PENETRATES THE FOUNDATIONS. I FEAR THAT THE SUBSIDENCE WILL RETURN, AND I WILL COLLAPSE INTO A PILE OF RUBBLE.
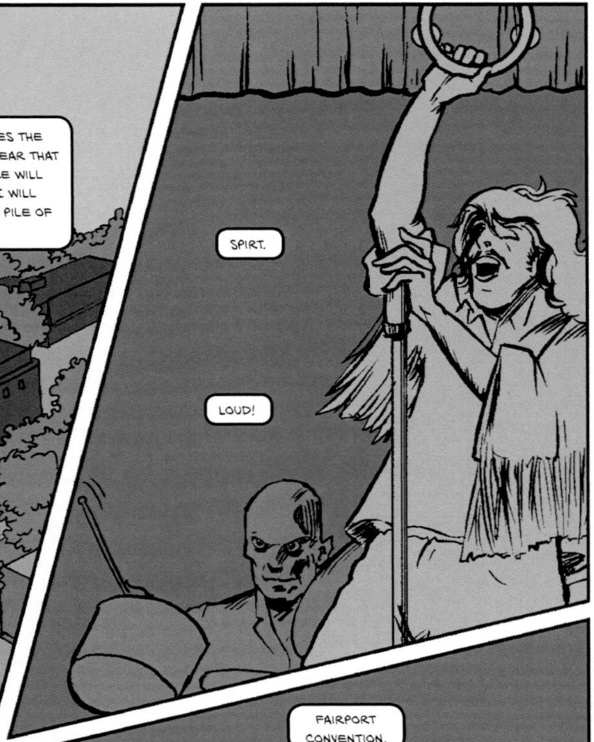
SPIRT.
LOUD!
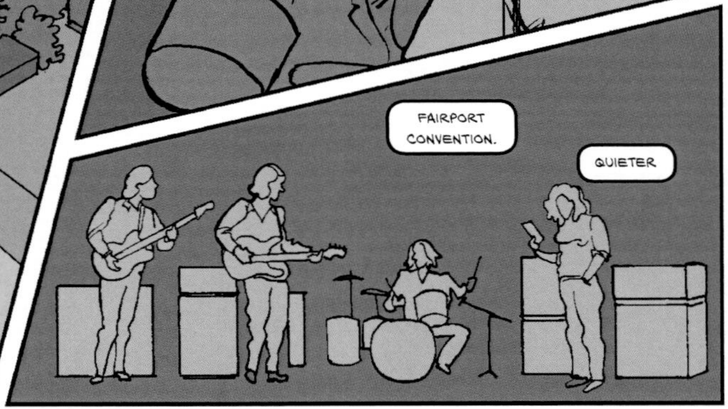
FAIRPORT CONVENTION.
QUIETER

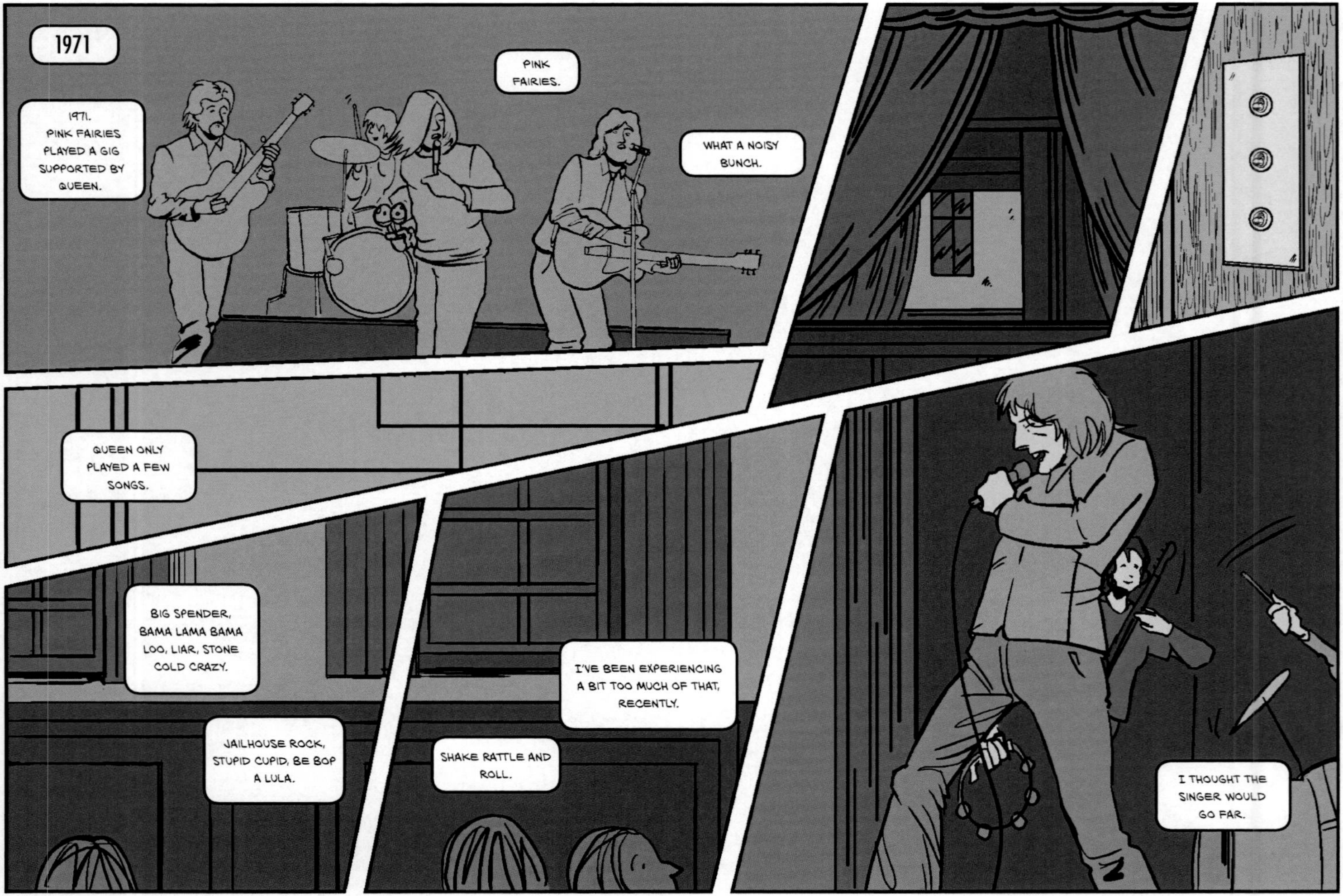
1971
1971. PINK FAIRIES PLAYED A GIG SUPPORTED BY QUEEN.
PINK FAIRIES.
WHAT A NOISY BUNCH.
QUEEN ONLY PLAYED A FEW SONGS.
BIG SPENDER, BAMA LAMA BAMA LOO, LIAR, STONE COLD CRAZY.
JAILHOUSE ROCK, STUPID CUPID, BE BOP A LULA.
SHAKE RATTLE AND ROLL.
I'VE BEEN EXPERIENCING A BIT TOO MUCH OF THAT, RECENTLY.
I THOUGHT THE SINGER WOULD GO FAR.

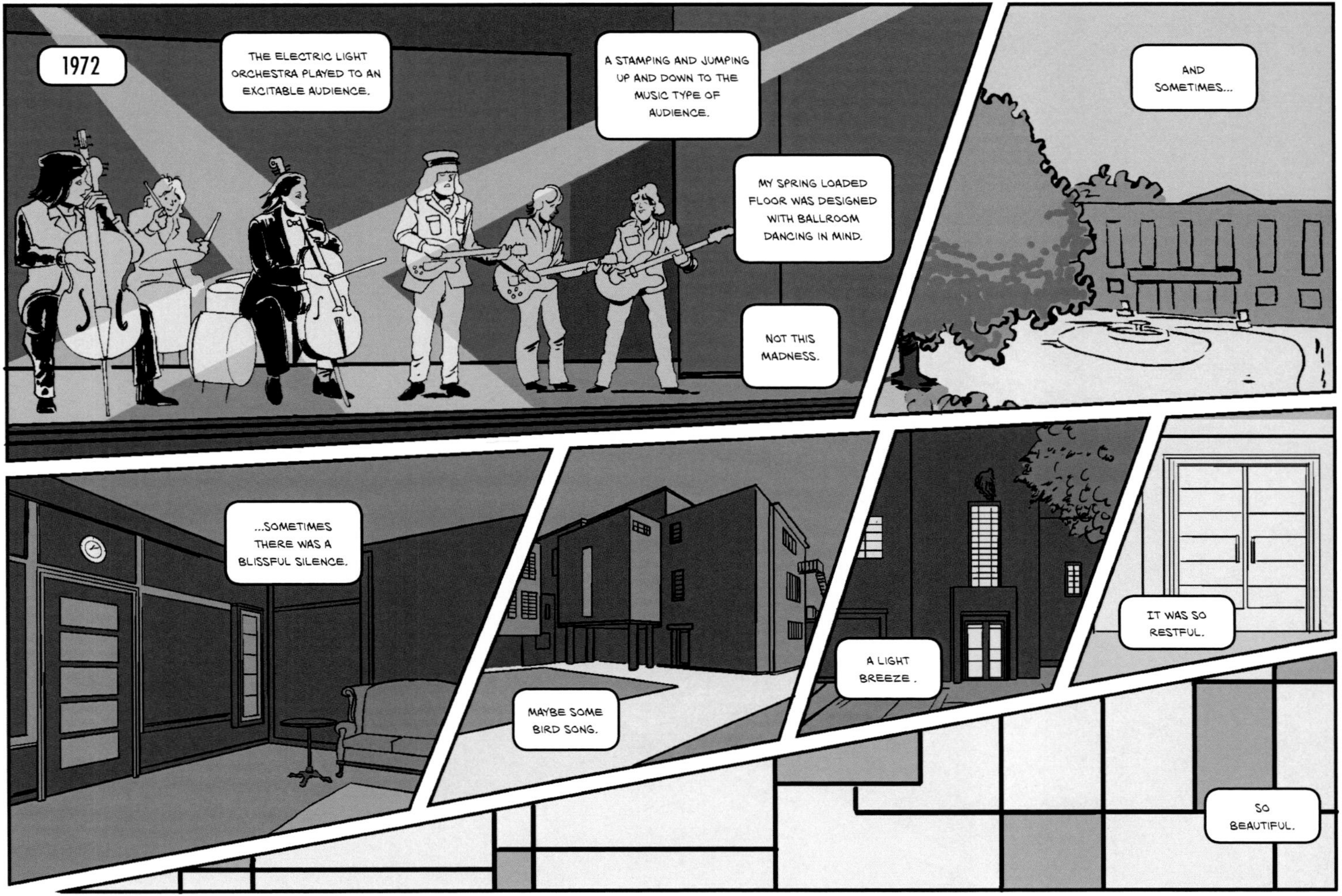
1972
THE ELECTRIC LIGHT ORCHESTRA PLAYED TO AN EXCITABLE AUDIENCE.
A STAMPING AND JUMPING UP AND DOWN TO THE MUSIC TYPE OF AUDIENCE.
MY SPRING LOADED FLOOR WAS DESIGNED WITH BALLROOM DANCING IN MIND.
NOT THIS MADNESS.
AND SOMETIMES...
...SOMETIMES THERE WAS A BLISSFUL SILENCE.
MAYBE SOME BIRD SONG.
A LIGHT BREEZE.
IT WAS SO RESTFUL.
SO BEAUTIFUL.

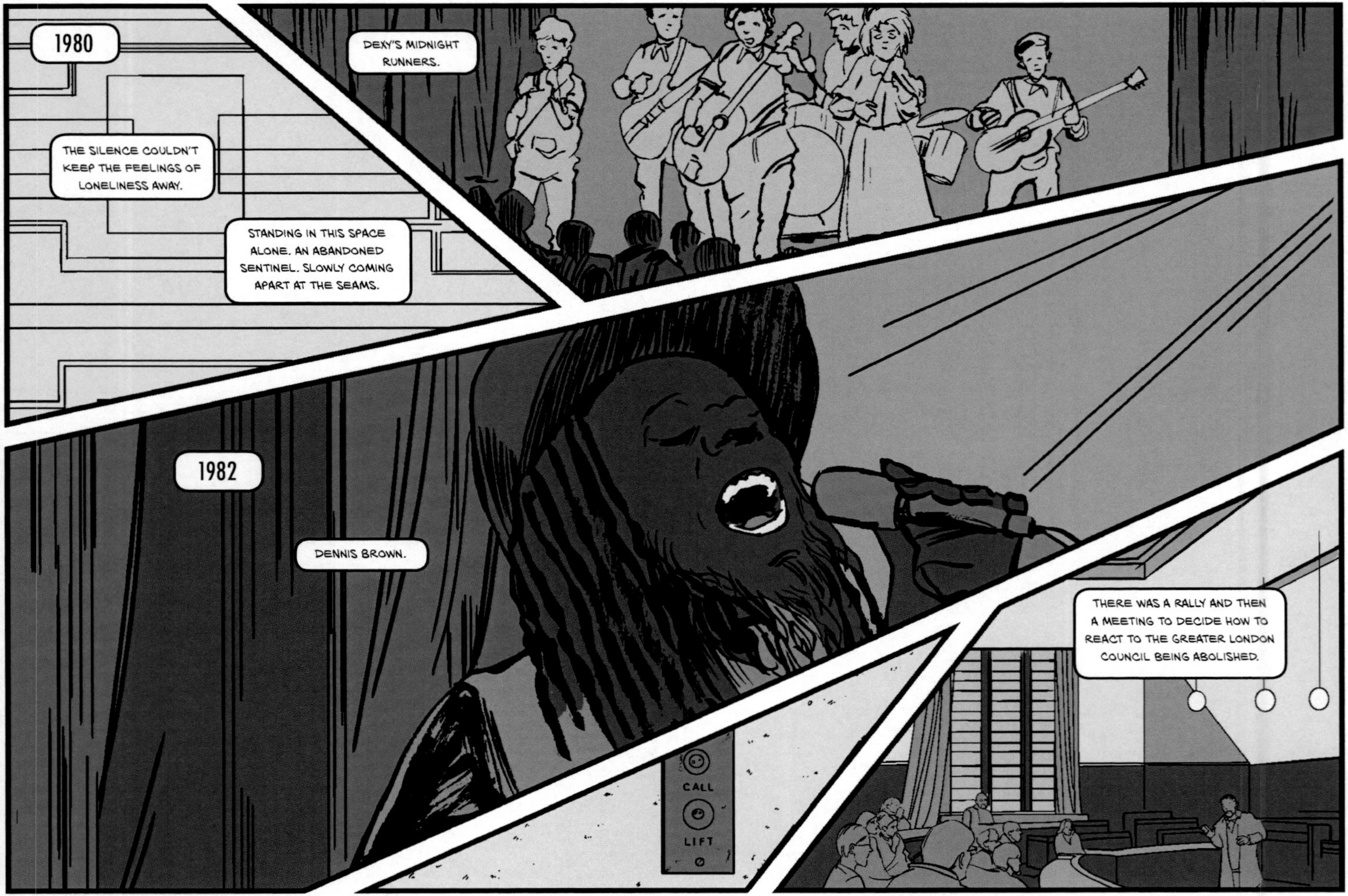
1980
THE SILENCE COULDN'T KEEP THE FEELINGS OF LONELINESS AWAY.
STANDING IN THIS SPACE ALONE. AN ABANDONED SENTINEL. SLOWLY COMING APART AT THE SEAMS.
DEXY'S MIDNIGHT RUNNERS.
1982
DENNIS BROWN.
CALL
LIFT
THERE WAS A RALLY AND THEN A MEETING TO DECIDE HOW TO REACT TO THE GREATER LONDON COUNCIL BEING ABOLISHED.

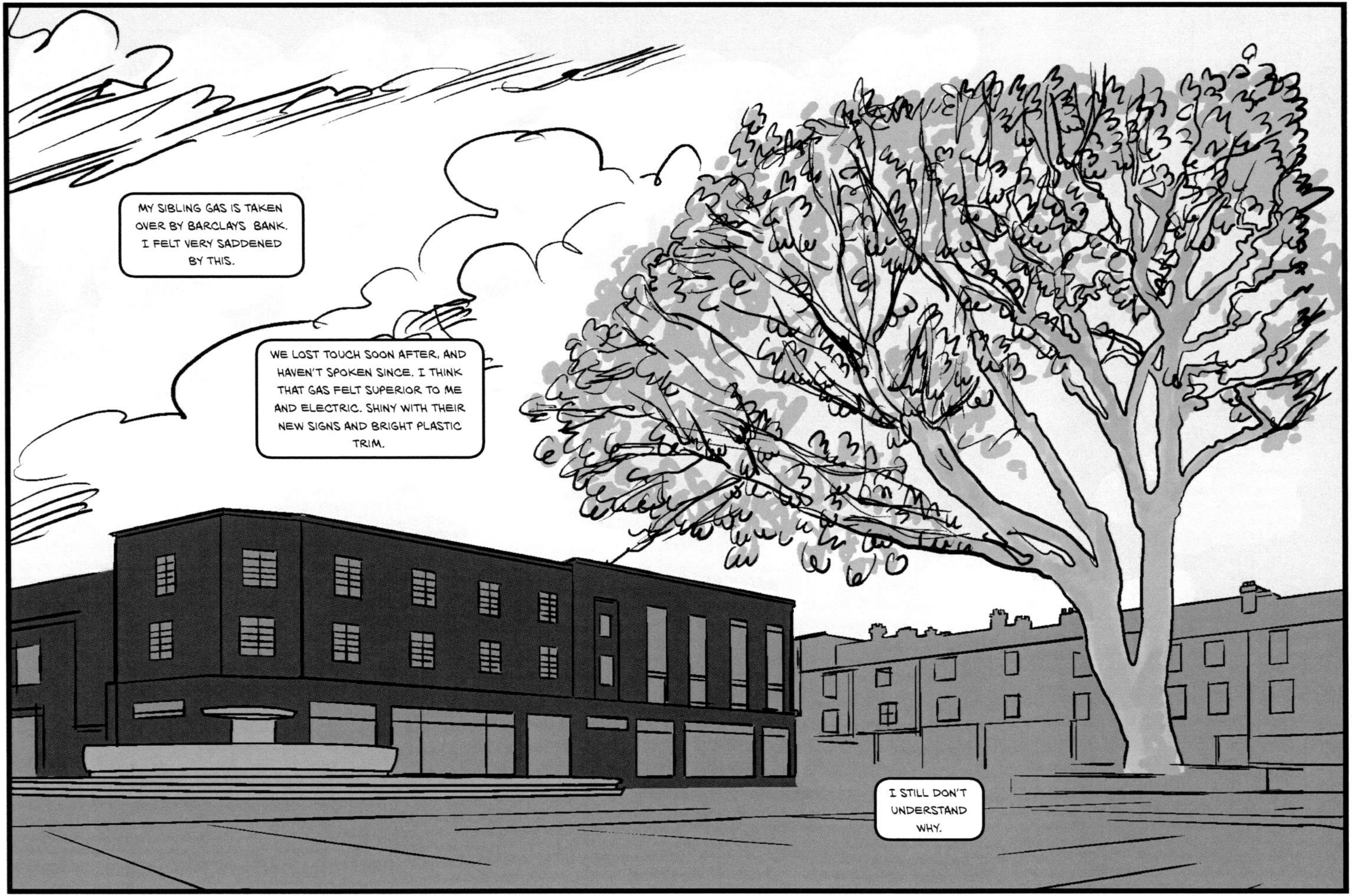
MY SIBLING GAS IS TAKEN OVER BY BARCLAYS BANK. I FELT VERY SADDENED BY THIS.
WE LOST TOUCH SOON AFTER, AND HAVEN'T SPOKEN SINCE. I THINK THAT GAS FELT SUPERIOR TO ME AND ELECTRIC. SHINY WITH THEIR NEW SIGNS AND BRIGHT PLASTIC TRIM.
I STILL DON'T UNDERSTAND WHY.

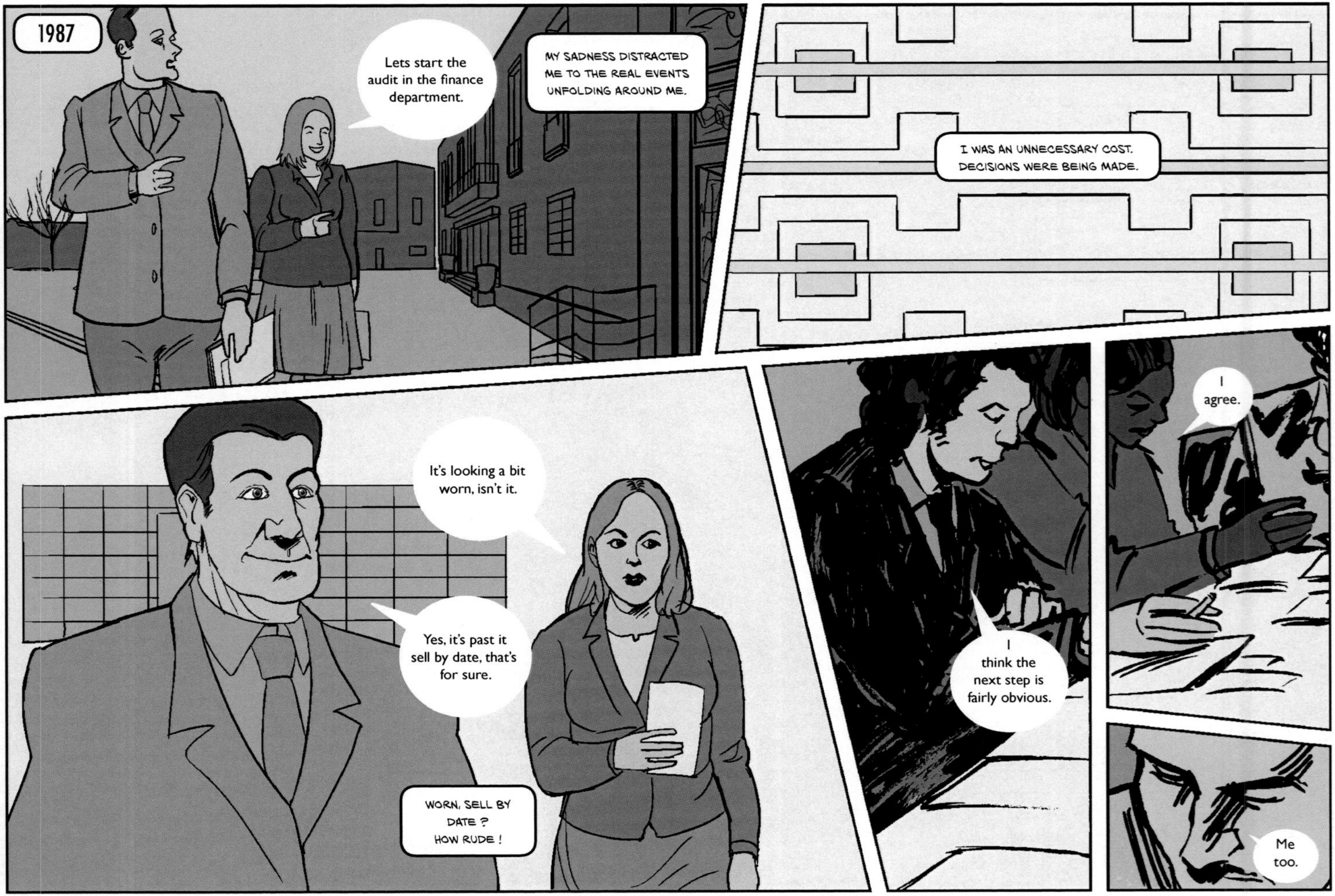
1987
Lets start the audit in the finance department.
MY SADNESS DISTRACTED ME TO THE REAL EVENTS UNFOLDING AROUND ME.
I WAS AN UNNECESSARY COST. DECISIONS WERE BEING MADE.
It's looking a bit worn, isn't it.
Yes, it's past it sell by date, that's for sure.
WORN, SELL BY DATE ? HOW RUDE !
I think the next step is fairly obvious.
I agree.
Me too.

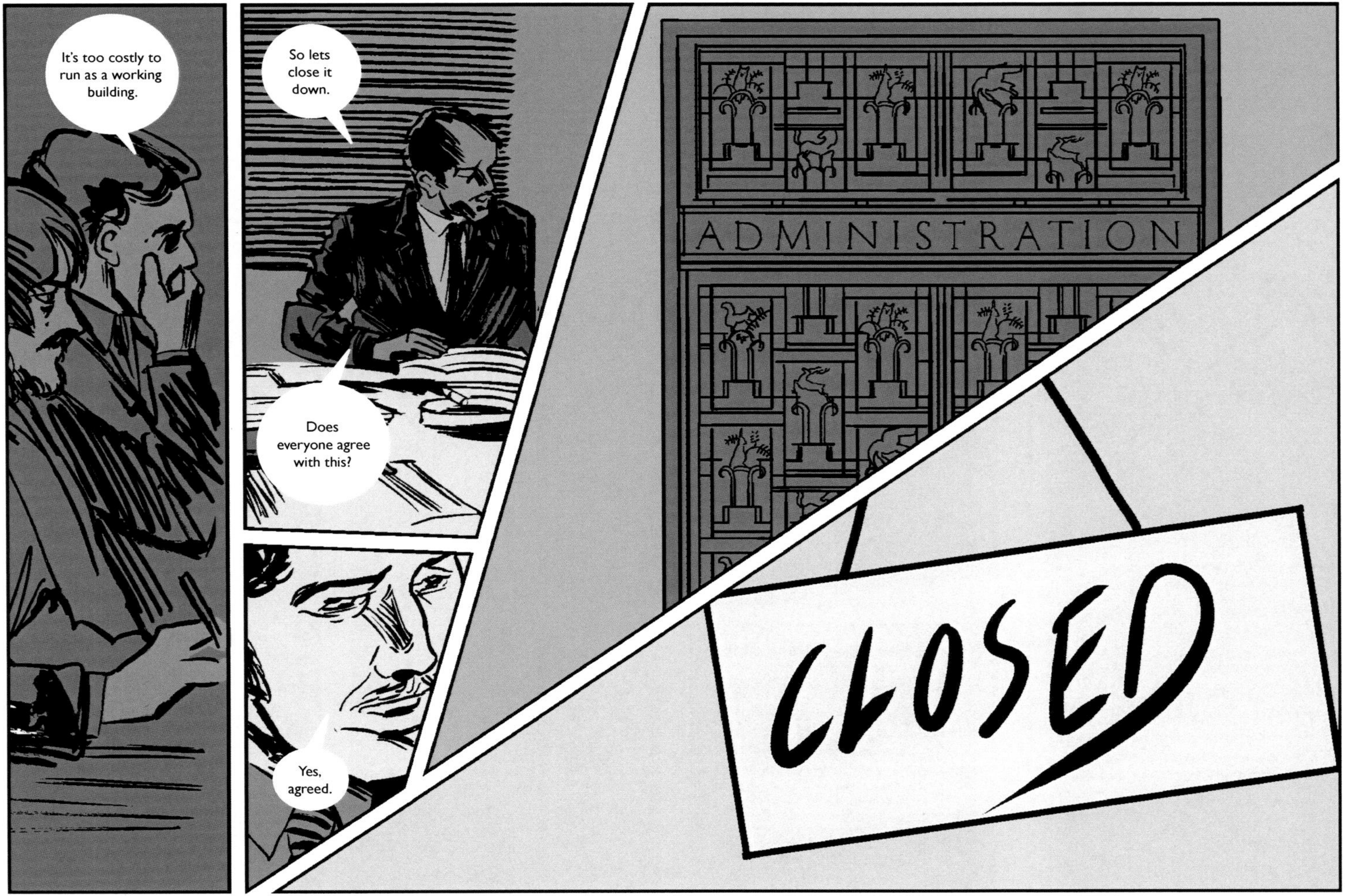
It's too costly to run as a working building.
So lets close it down.
Does everyone agree with this?
Yes, agreed.
ADMINISTRATION
CLOSED

I'VE HAD ENOUGH. I'M GOING TO SLEEP.

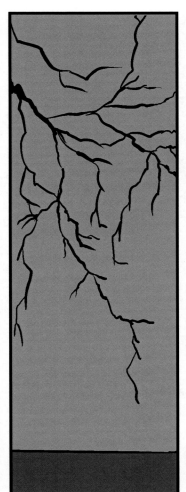

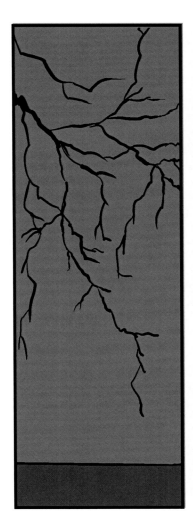

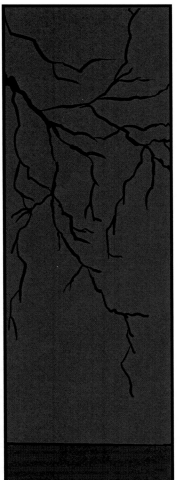

GOOD NIGHT.

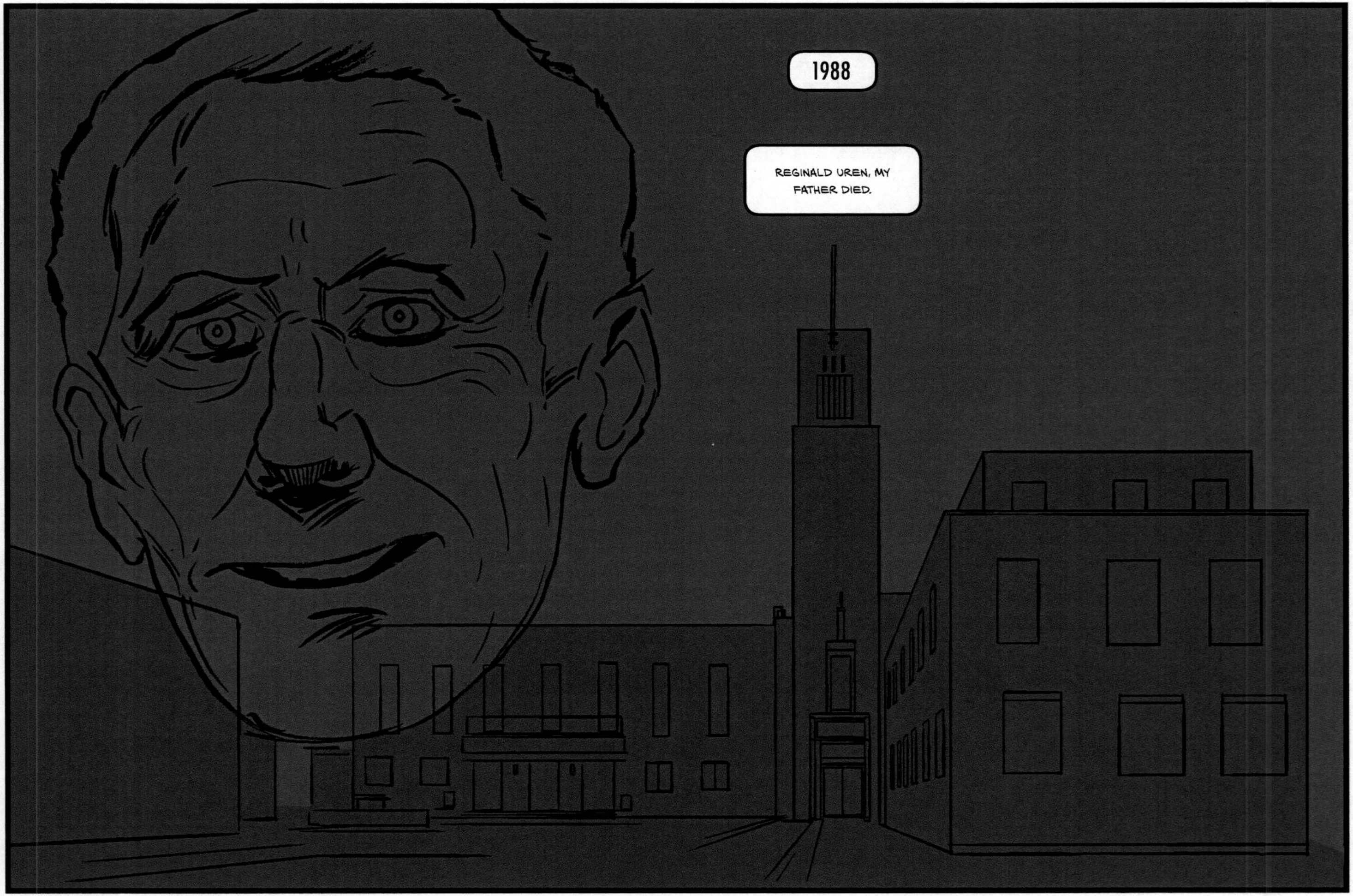
1988
REGINALD UREN, MY FATHER DIED.

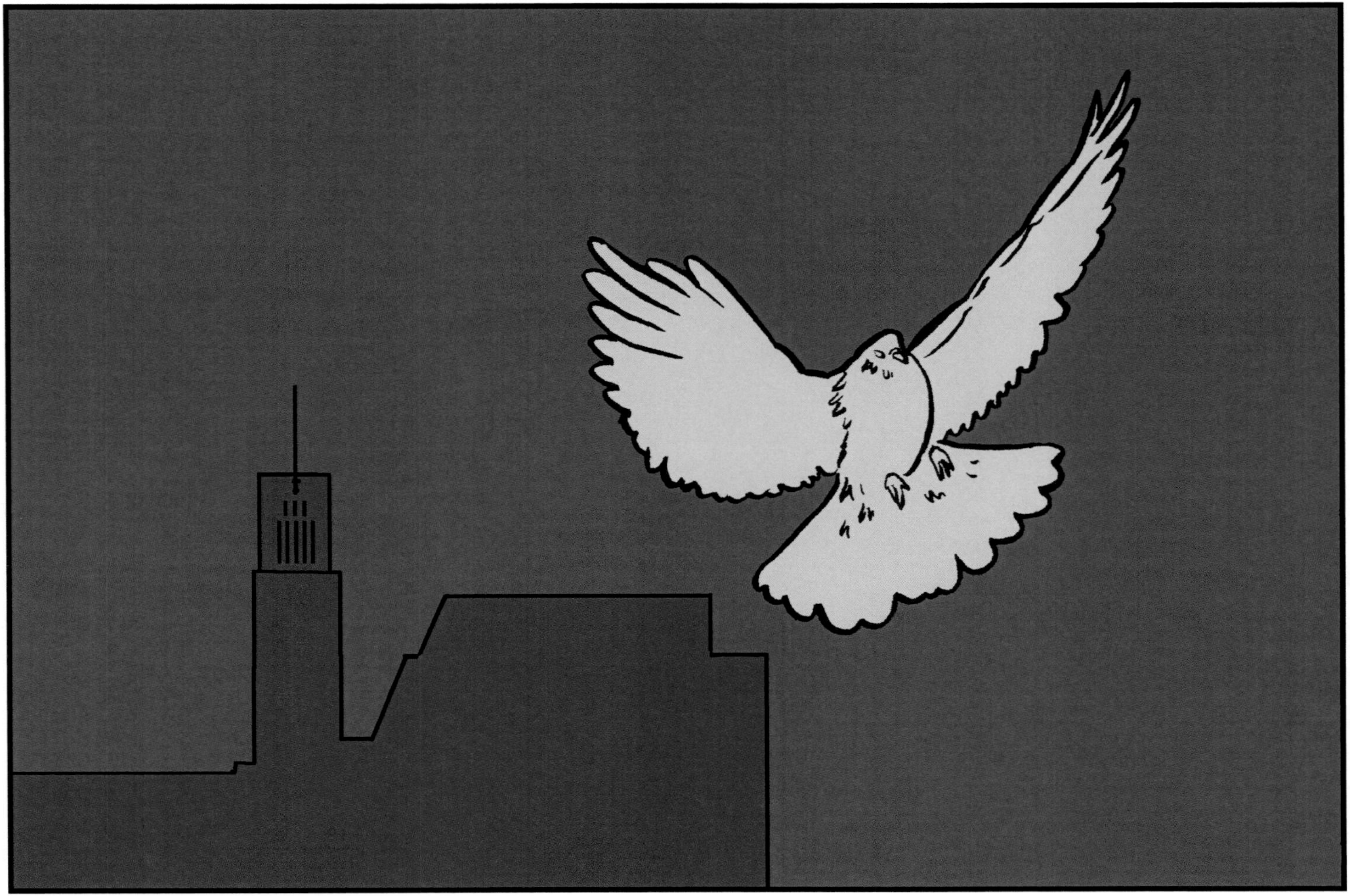

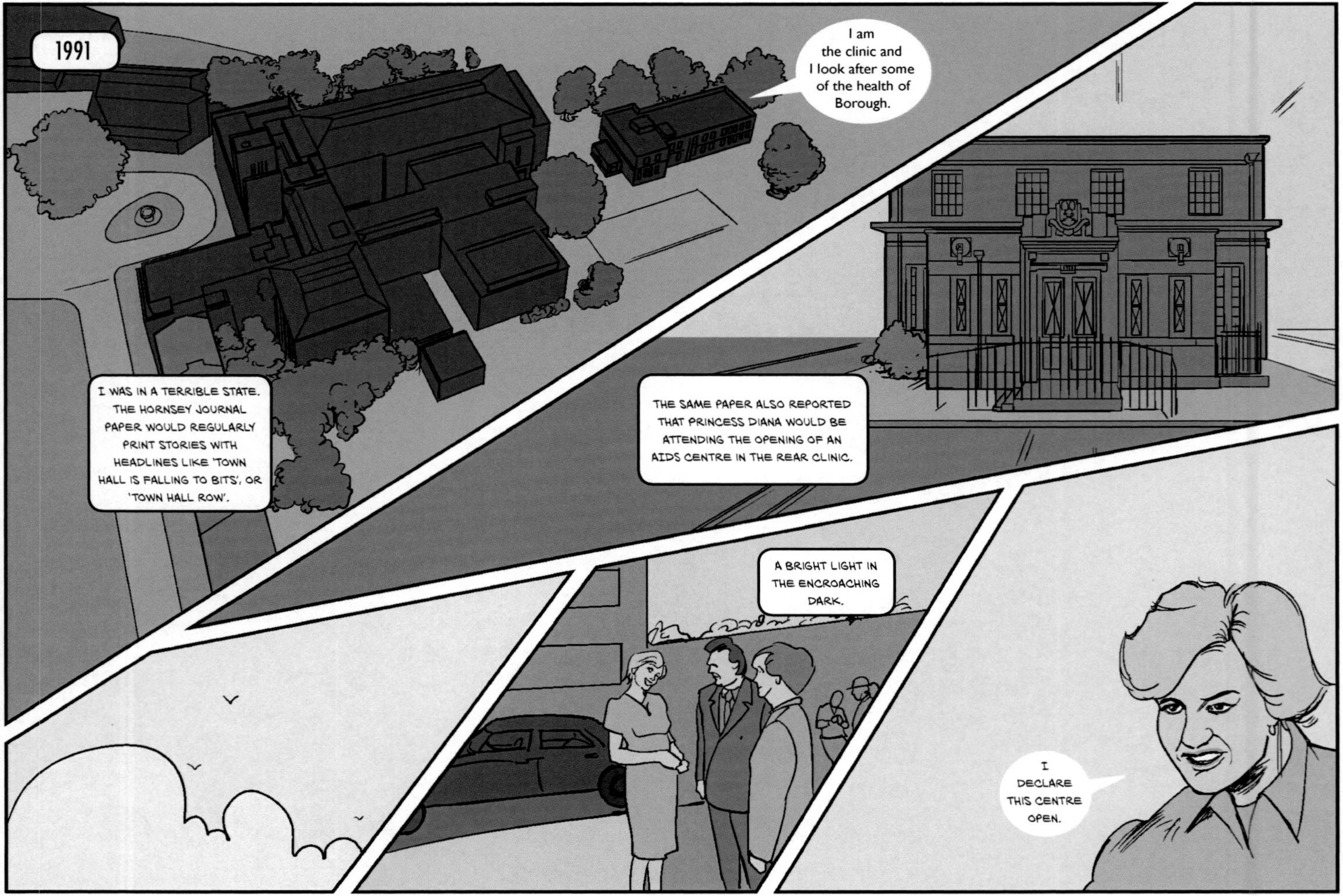
1991
I am the clinic and I look after some of the health of Borough.
I WAS IN A TERRIBLE STATE. THE HORNSEY JOURNAL PAPER WOULD REGULARLY PRINT STORIES WITH HEADLINES LIKE 'TOWN HALL IS FALLING TO BITS', OR 'TOWN HALL ROW'.
THE SAME PAPER ALSO REPORTED THAT PRINCESS DIANA WOULD BE ATTENDING THE OPENING OF AN AIDS CENTRE IN THE REAR CLINIC.
A BRIGHT LIGHT IN THE ENCROACHING DARK.
I DECLARE THIS CENTRE OPEN.

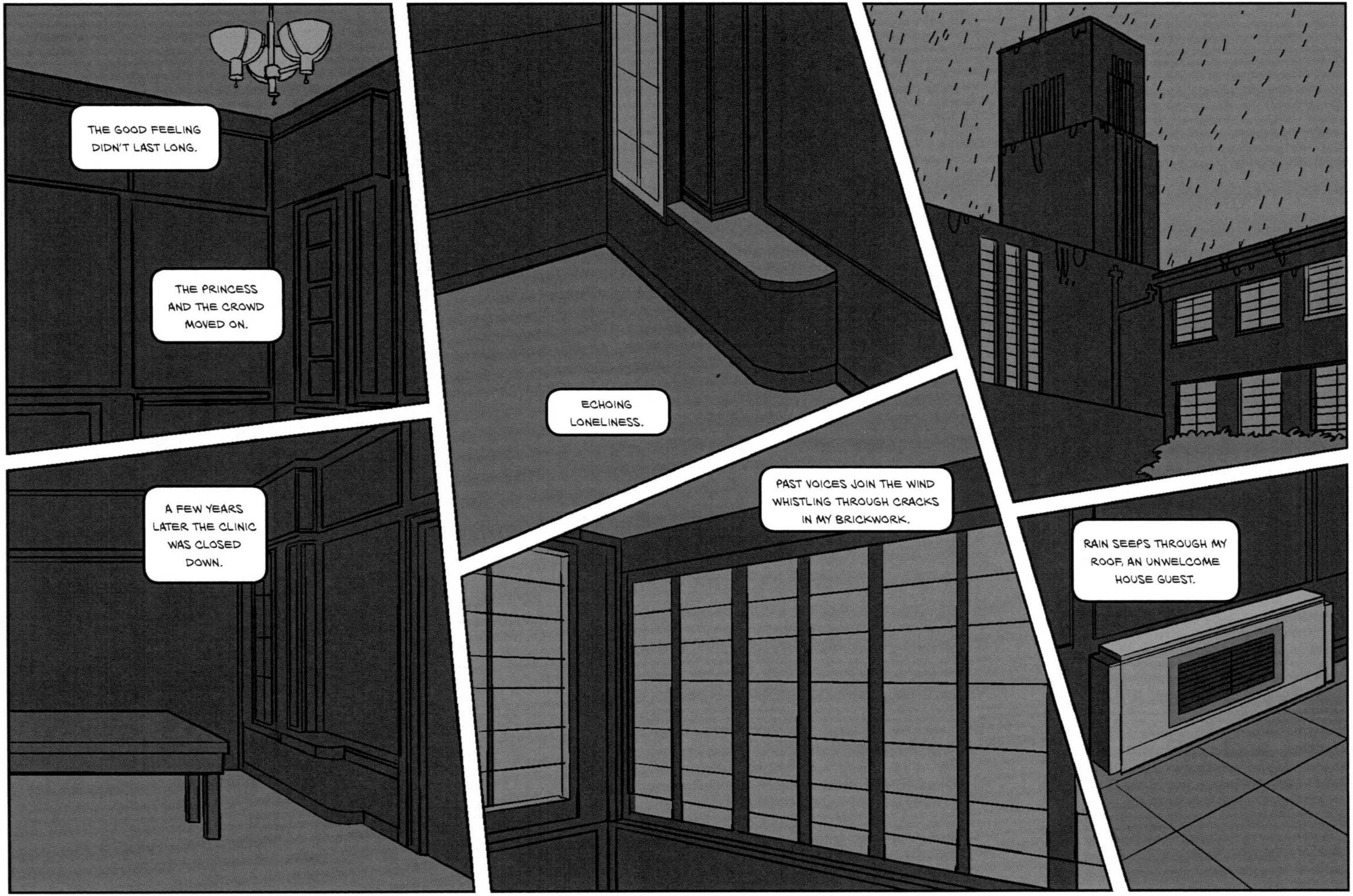
THE GOOD FEELING DIDN'T LAST LONG.
THE PRINCESS AND THE CROWD MOVED ON.
A FEW YEARS LATER THE CLINIC WAS CLOSED DOWN.
ECHOING LONELINESS.
PAST VOICES JOIN THE WIND WHISTLING THROUGH CRACKS IN MY BRICKWORK.
RAIN SEEPS THROUGH MY ROOF, AN UNWELCOME HOUSE GUEST.

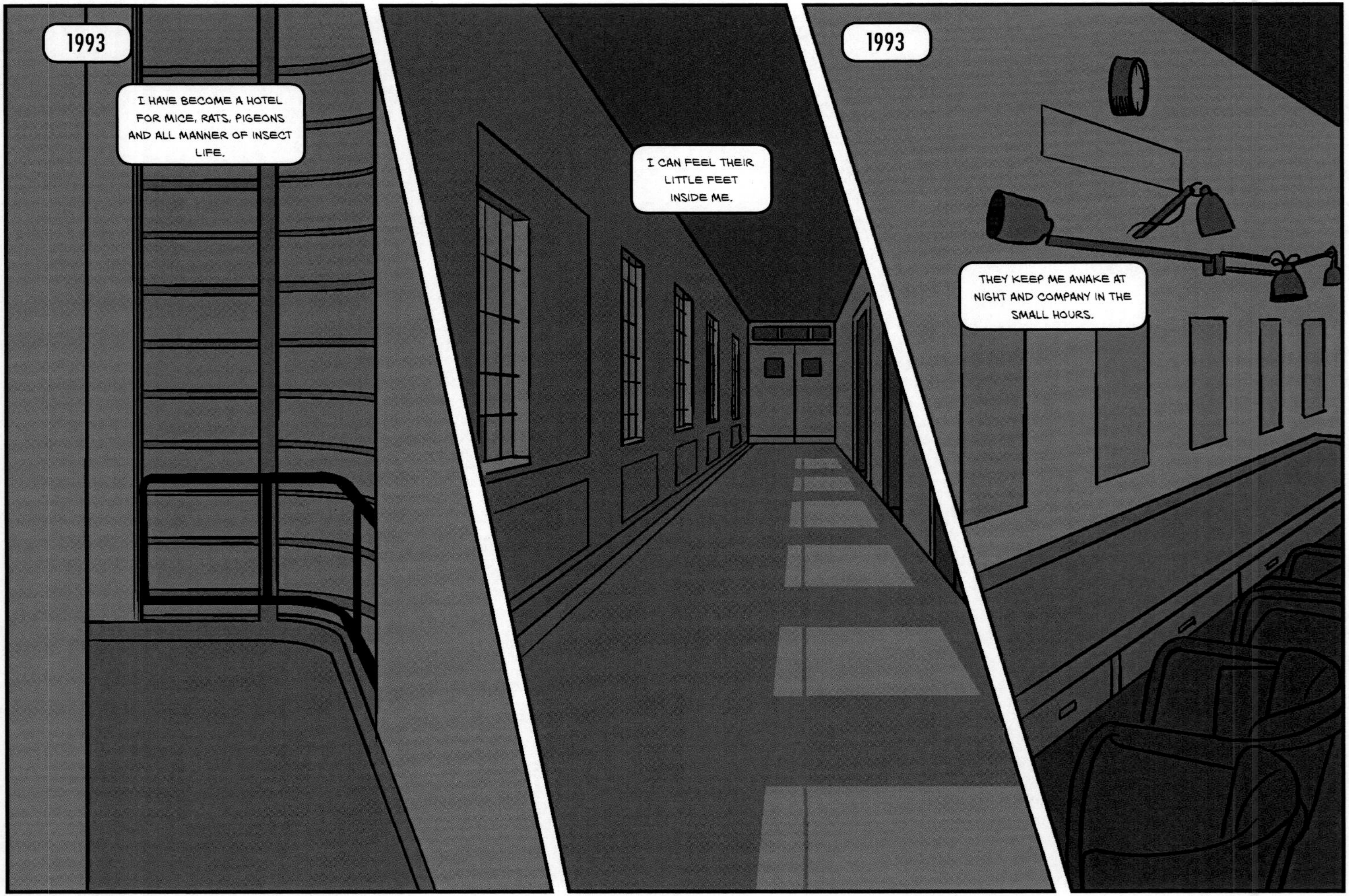
1993
I HAVE BECOME A HOTEL FOR MICE, RATS, PIGEONS AND ALL MANNER OF INSECT LIFE.
I CAN FEEL THEIR LITTLE FEET INSIDE ME.
1993
THEY KEEP ME AWAKE AT NIGHT AND COMPANY IN THE SMALL HOURS.

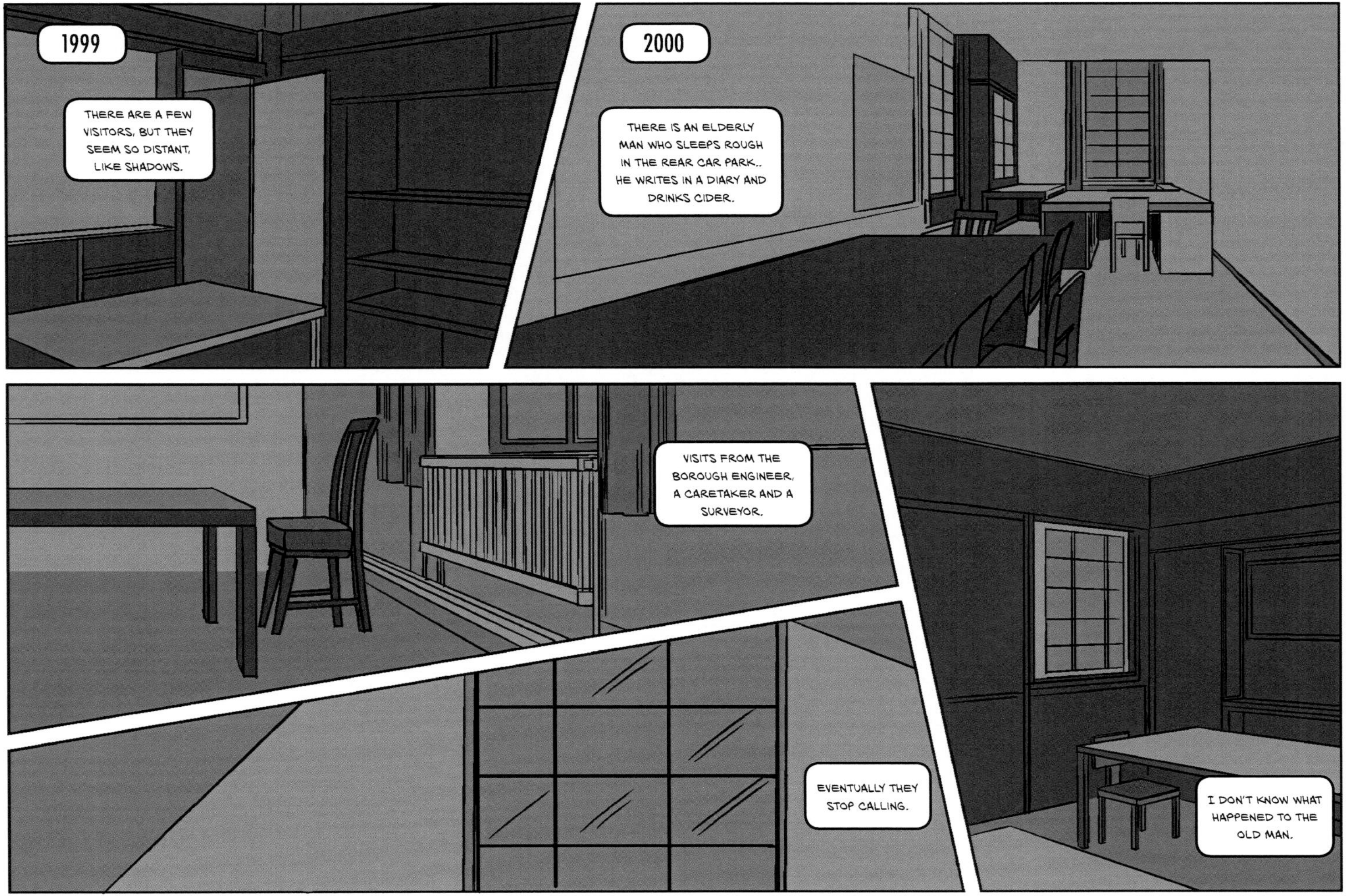
1999
THERE ARE A FEW VISITORS, BUT THEY SEEM SO DISTANT, LIKE SHADOWS.
2000
THERE IS AN ELDERLY MAN WHO SLEEPS ROUGH IN THE REAR CAR PARK.. HE WRITES IN A DIARY AND DRINKS CIDER.
VISITS FROM THE BOROUGH ENGINEER, A CARETAKER AND A SURVEYOR.
EVENTUALLY THEY STOP CALLING.
I DON'T KNOW WHAT HAPPENED TO THE OLD MAN.

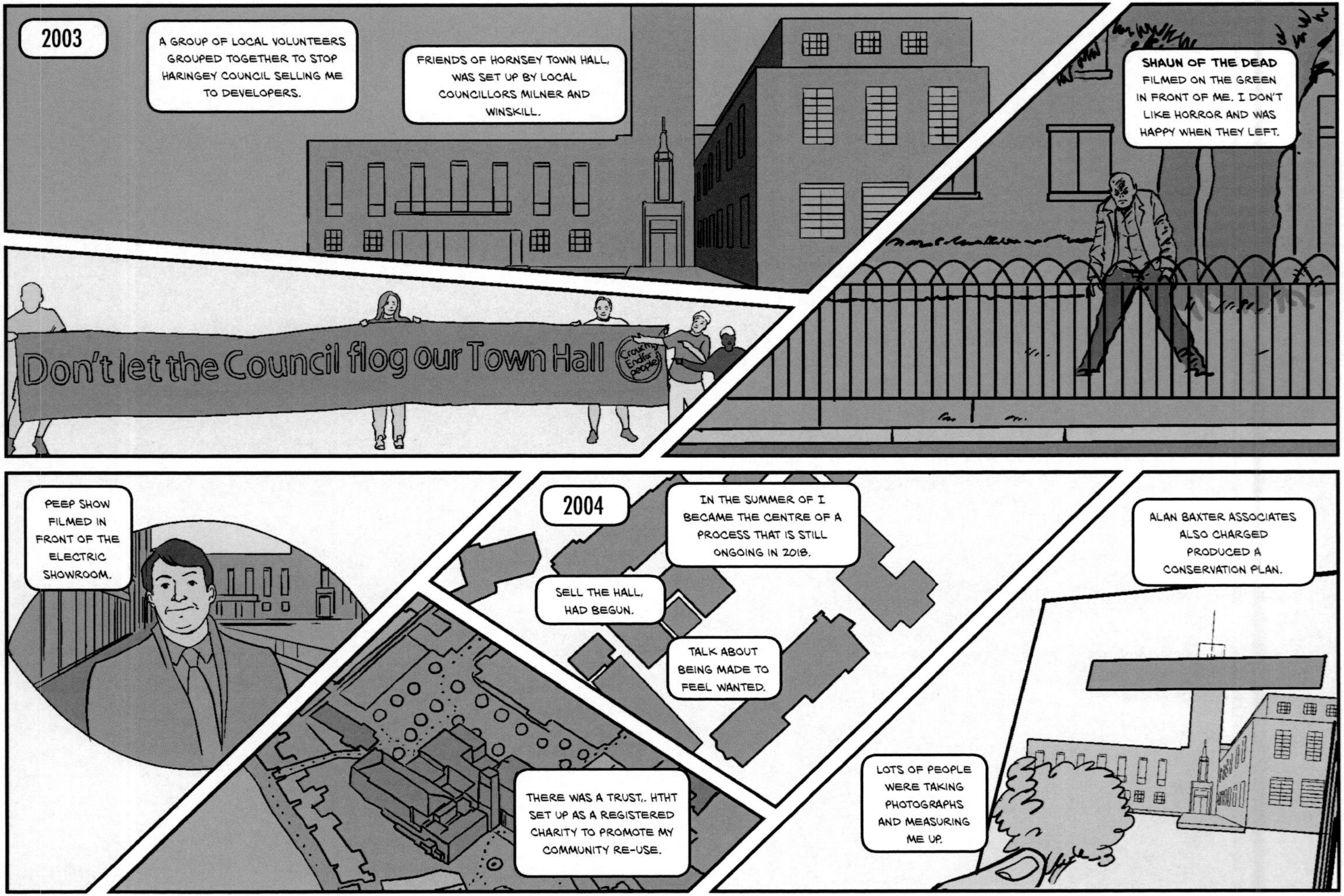
2003
A GROUP OF LOCAL VOLUNTEERS GROUPED TOGETHER TO STOP HARINGEY COUNCIL SELLING ME TO DEVELOPERS.
FRIENDS OF HORNSEY TOWN HALL, WAS SET UP BY LOCAL COUNCILLORS MILNER AND WINSKILL.
SHAUN OF THE DEAD FILMED ON THE GREEN IN FRONT OF ME. I DON'T LIKE HORROR AND WAS HAPPY WHEN THEY LEFT.
Don't let the Council flog our Town Hall
PEEP SHOW FILMED IN FRONT OF THE ELECTRIC SHOWROOM.
2004
IN THE SUMMER OF I BECAME THE CENTRE OF A PROCESS THAT IS STILL ONGOING IN 2018.
SELL THE HALL, HAD BEGUN.
TALK ABOUT BEING MADE TO FEEL WANTED.
THERE WAS A TRUST,. HTHT SET UP AS A REGISTERED CHARITY TO PROMOTE MY COMMUNITY RE-USE.
ALAN BAXTER ASSOCIATES ALSO CHARGED PRODUCED A CONSERVATION PLAN.
LOTS OF PEOPLE WERE TAKING PHOTOGRAPHS AND MEASURING ME UP.

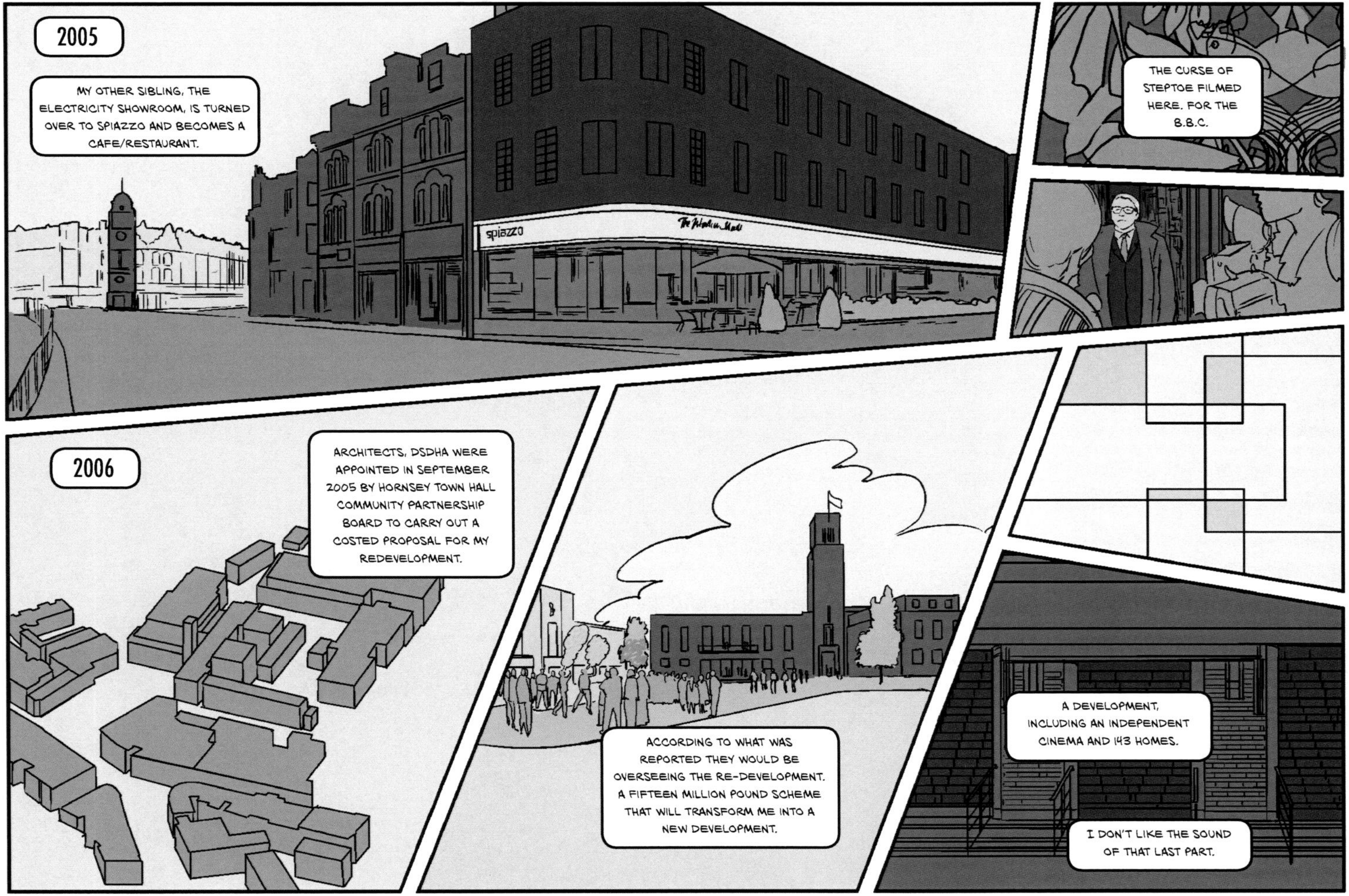
2005
MY OTHER SIBLING, THE ELECTRICITY SHOWROOM, IS TURNED OVER TO SPIAZZO AND BECOMES A CAFE/RESTAURANT.
spiazzo
THE CURSE OF STEPTOE FILMED HERE. FOR THE B.B.C.
2006
ARCHITECTS, DSDHA WERE APPOINTED IN SEPTEMBER 2005 BY HORNSEY TOWN HALL COMMUNITY PARTNERSHIP BOARD TO CARRY OUT A COSTED PROPOSAL FOR MY REDEVELOPMENT.
ACCORDING TO WHAT WAS REPORTED THEY WOULD BE OVERSEEING THE RE-DEVELOPMENT. A FIFTEEN MILLION POUND SCHEME THAT WILL TRANSFORM ME INTO A NEW DEVELOPMENT.
A DEVELOPMENT, INCLUDING AN INDEPENDENT CINEMA AND 143 HOMES.
I DON'T LIKE THE SOUND OF THAT LAST PART.

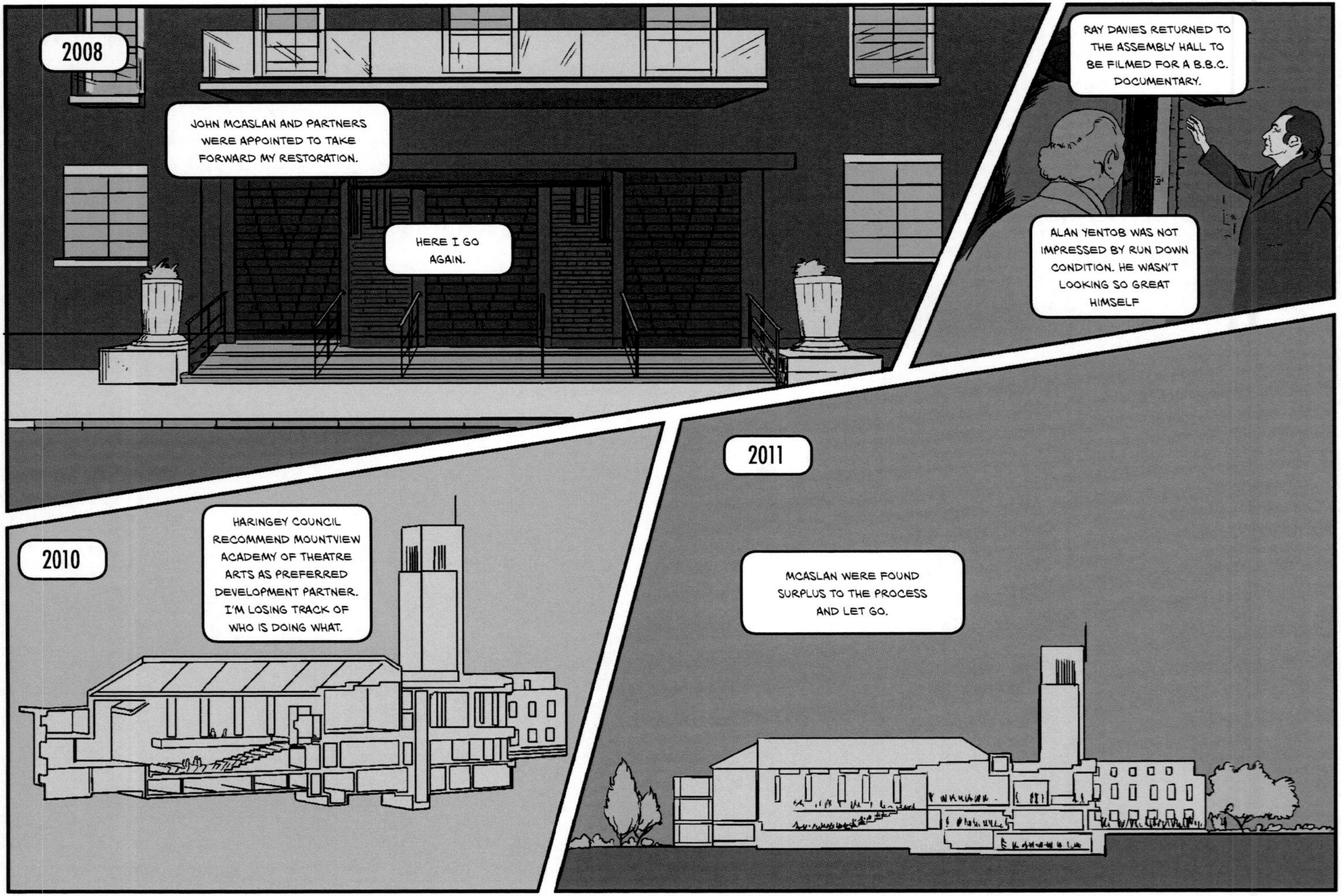
2008
JOHN MCASLAN AND PARTNERS WERE APPOINTED TO TAKE FORWARD MY RESTORATION.
HERE I GO AGAIN.
RAY DAVIES RETURNED TO THE ASSEMBLY HALL TO BE FILMED FOR A B.B.C. DOCUMENTARY.
ALAN YENTOB WAS NOT IMPRESSED BY RUN DOWN CONDITION. HE WASN'T LOOKING SO GREAT HIMSELF
2010
HARINGEY COUNCIL RECOMMEND MOUNTVIEW ACADEMY OF THEATRE ARTS AS PREFERRED DEVELOPMENT PARTNER. I'M LOSING TRACK OF WHO IS DOING WHAT.
2011
MCASLAN WERE FOUND SURPLUS TO THE PROCESS AND LET GO.

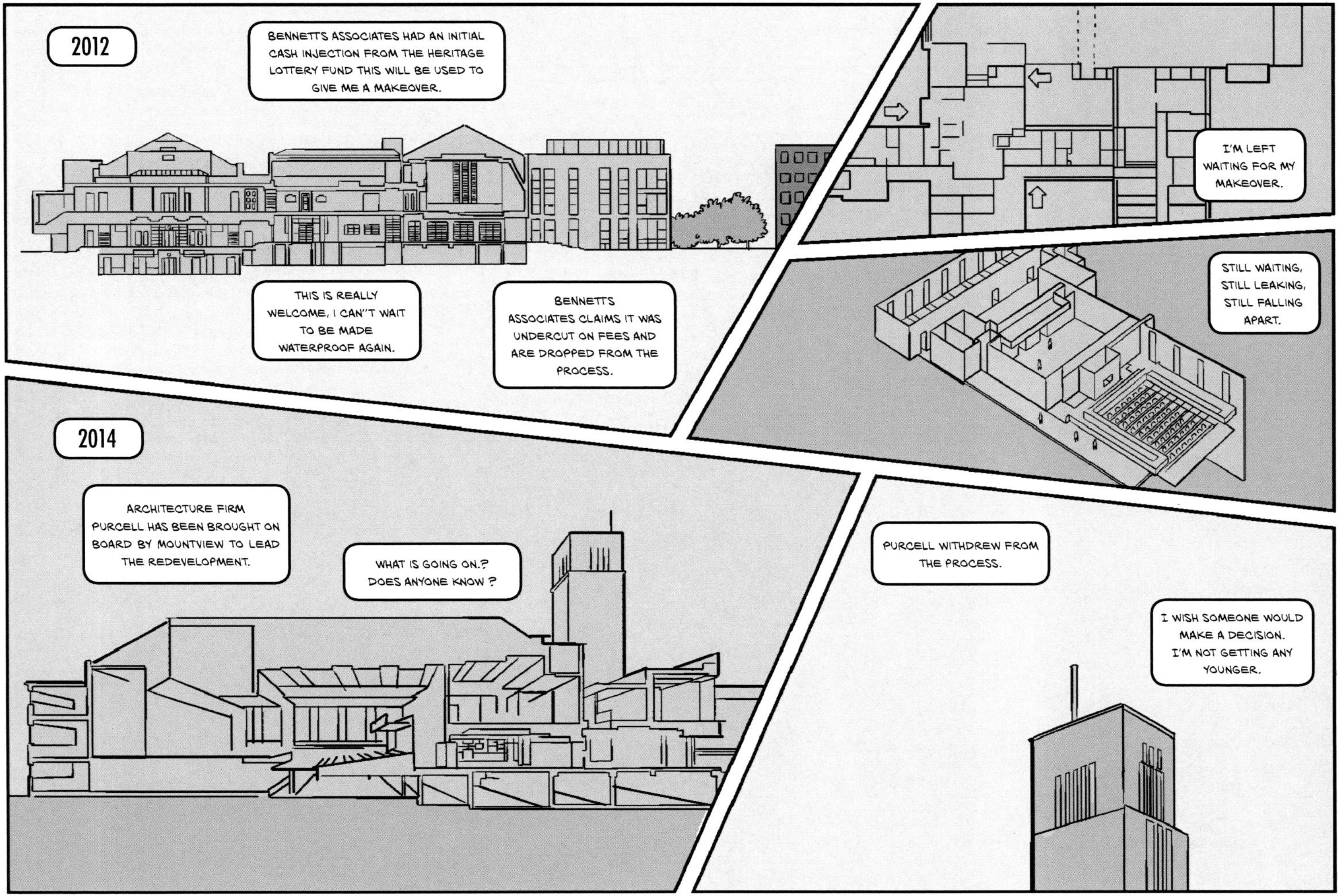
2012
BENNETTS ASSOCIATES HAD AN INITIAL CASH INJECTION FROM THE HERITAGE LOTTERY FUND THIS WILL BE USED TO GIVE ME A MAKEOVER.
THIS IS REALLY WELCOME, I CAN''T WAIT TO BE MADE WATERPROOF AGAIN.
BENNETTS ASSOCIATES CLAIMS IT WAS UNDERCUT ON FEES AND ARE DROPPED FROM THE PROCESS.
I'M LEFT WAITING FOR MY MAKEOVER.
STILL WAITING, STILL LEAKING, STILL FALLING APART.
2014
ARCHITECTURE FIRM PURCELL HAS BEEN BROUGHT ON BOARD BY MOUNTVIEW TO LEAD THE REDEVELOPMENT.
WHAT IS GOING ON.? DOES ANYONE KNOW ?
PURCELL WITHDREW FROM THE PROCESS.
I WISH SOMEONE WOULD MAKE A DECISION. I'M NOT GETTING ANY YOUNGER.

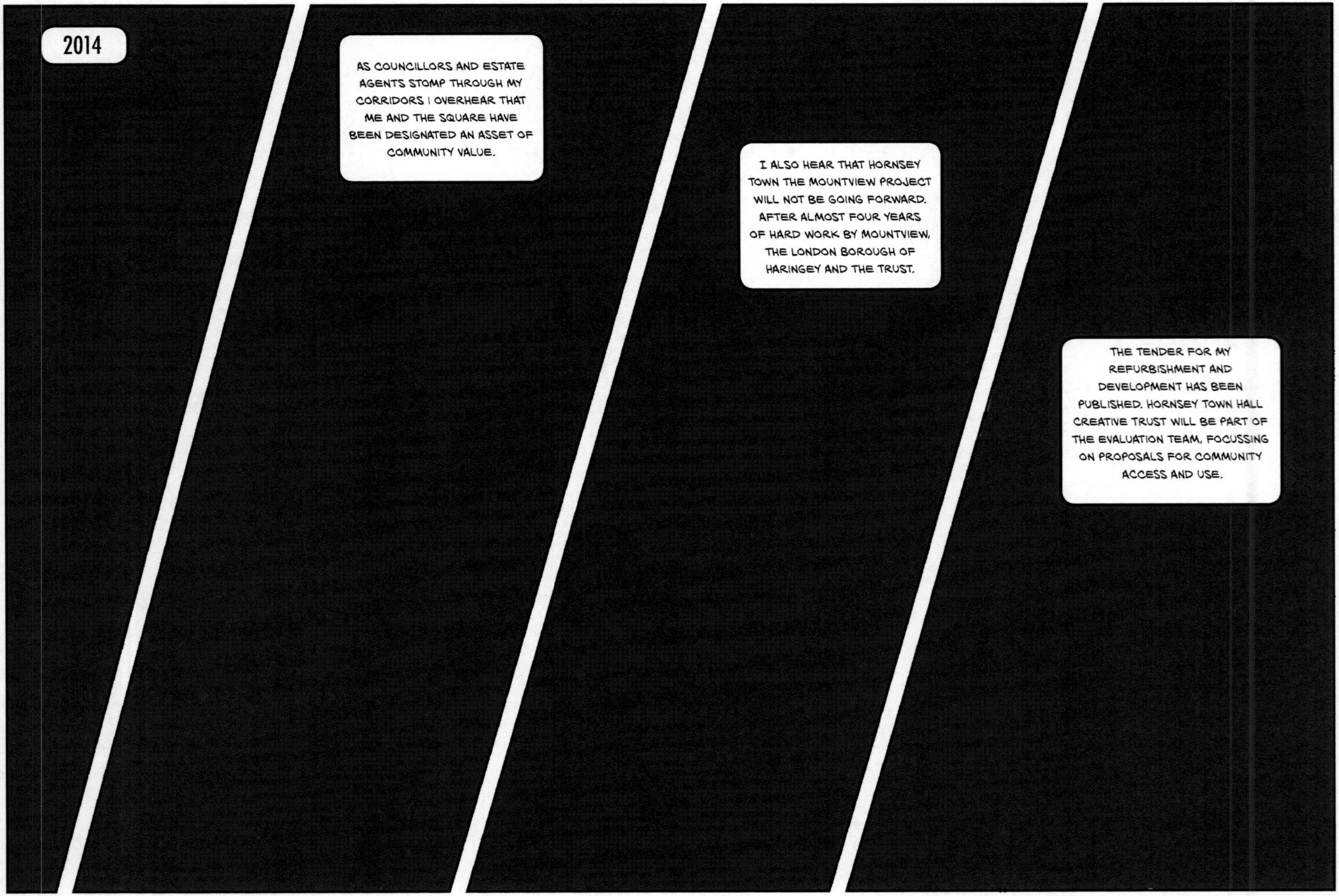
2014
AS COUNCILLORS AND ESTATE AGENTS STOMP THROUGH MY CORRIDORS I OVERHEAR THAT ME AND THE SQUARE HAVE BEEN DESIGNATED AN ASSET OF COMMUNITY VALUE.
I ALSO HEAR THAT HORNSEY TOWN THE MOUNTVIEW PROJECT WILL NOT BE GOING FORWARD. AFTER ALMOST FOUR YEARS OF HARD WORK BY MOUNTVIEW, THE LONDON BOROUGH OF HARINGEY AND THE TRUST.
THE TENDER FOR MY REFURBISHMENT AND DEVELOPMENT HAS BEEN PUBLISHED. HORNSEY TOWN HALL CREATIVE TRUST WILL BE PART OF THE EVALUATION TEAM, FOCUSSING ON PROPOSALS FOR COMMUNITY ACCESS AND USE.

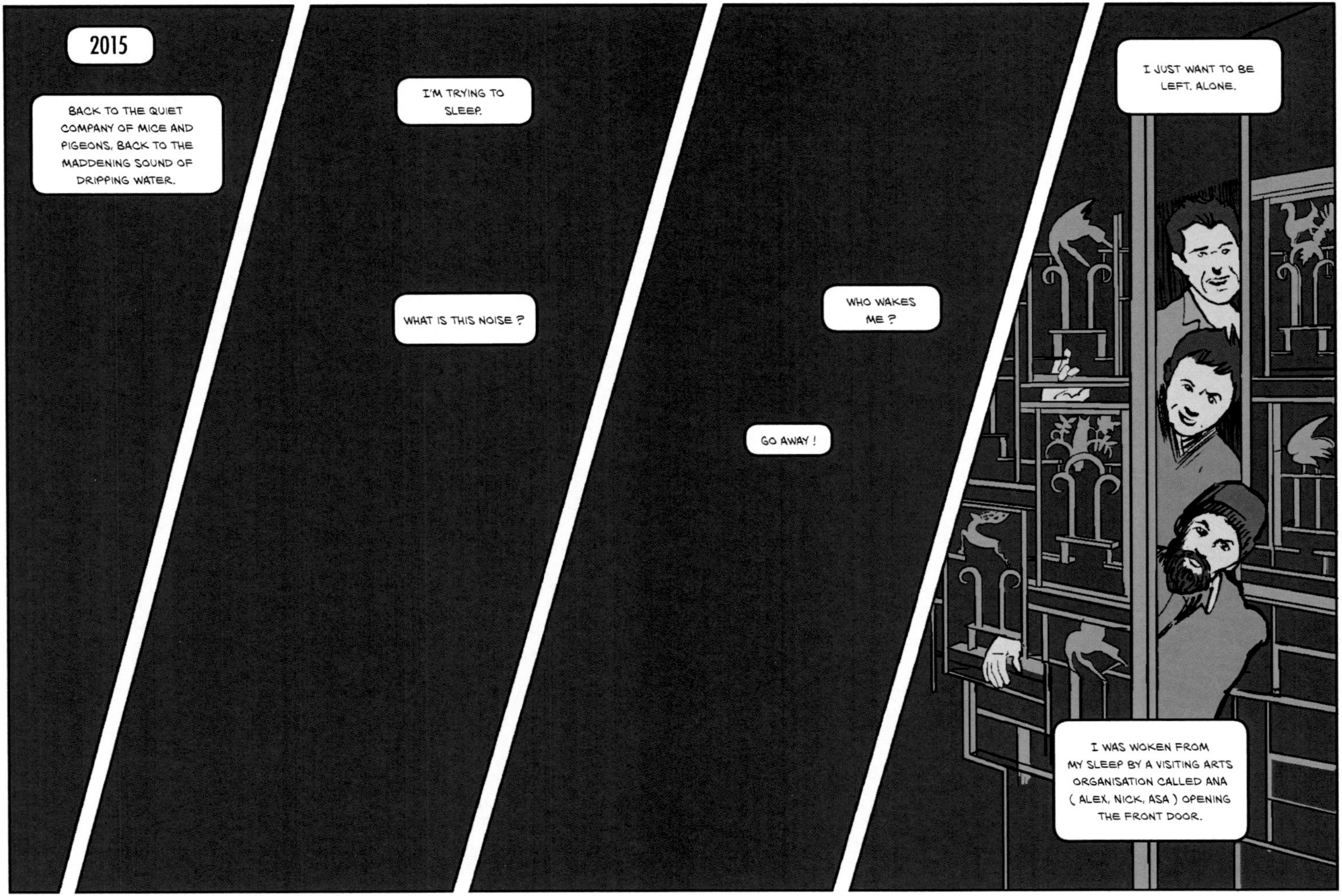
2015
BACK TO THE QUIET COMPANY OF MICE AND PIGEONS, BACK TO THE MADDENING SOUND OF DRIPPING WATER.
I'M TRYING TO SLEEP.
WHAT IS THIS NOISE ?
WHO WAKES ME ?
GO AWAY !
I JUST WANT TO BE LEFT. ALONE.
I WAS WOKEN FROM MY SLEEP BY A VISITING ARTS ORGANISATION CALLED ANA (ALEX, NICK, ASA) OPENING THE FRONT DOOR.

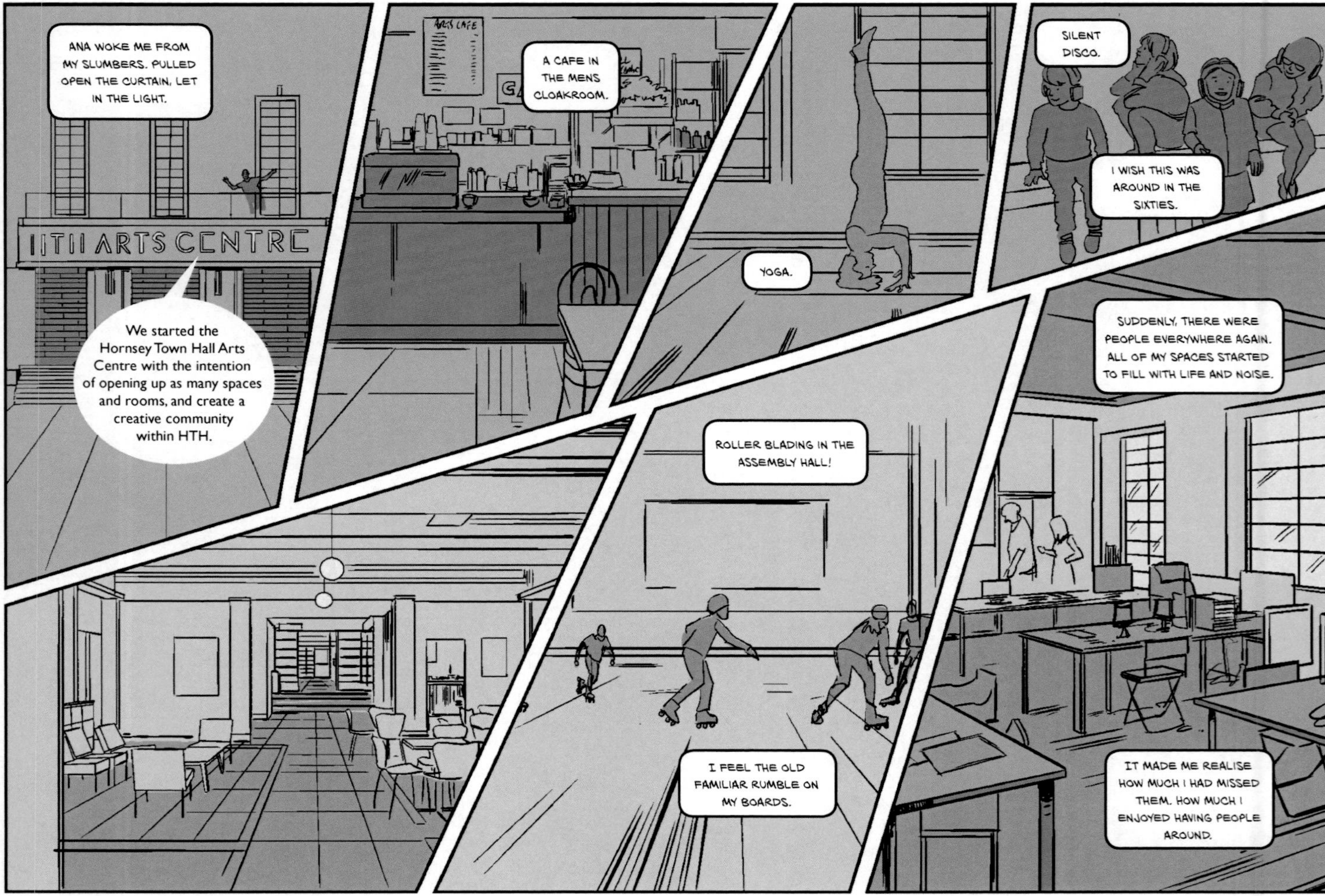
ANA WOKE ME FROM MY SLUMBERS. PULLED OPEN THE CURTAIN, LET IN THE LIGHT.
HTH ARTS CENTRE
We started the Hornsey Town Hall Arts Centre with the intention of opening up as many spaces and rooms, and create a creative community within HTH.
A CAFE IN THE MENS CLOAKROOM.
YOGA.
SILENT DISCO.
I WISH THIS WAS AROUND IN THE SIXTIES.
SUDDENLY, THERE WERE PEOPLE EVERYWHERE AGAIN. ALL OF MY SPACES STARTED TO FILL WITH LIFE AND NOISE.
ROLLER BLADING IN THE ASSEMBLY HALL!
I FEEL THE OLD FAMILIAR RUMBLE ON MY BOARDS.
IT MADE ME REALISE HOW MUCH I HAD MISSED THEM. HOW MUCH I ENJOYED HAVING PEOPLE AROUND.

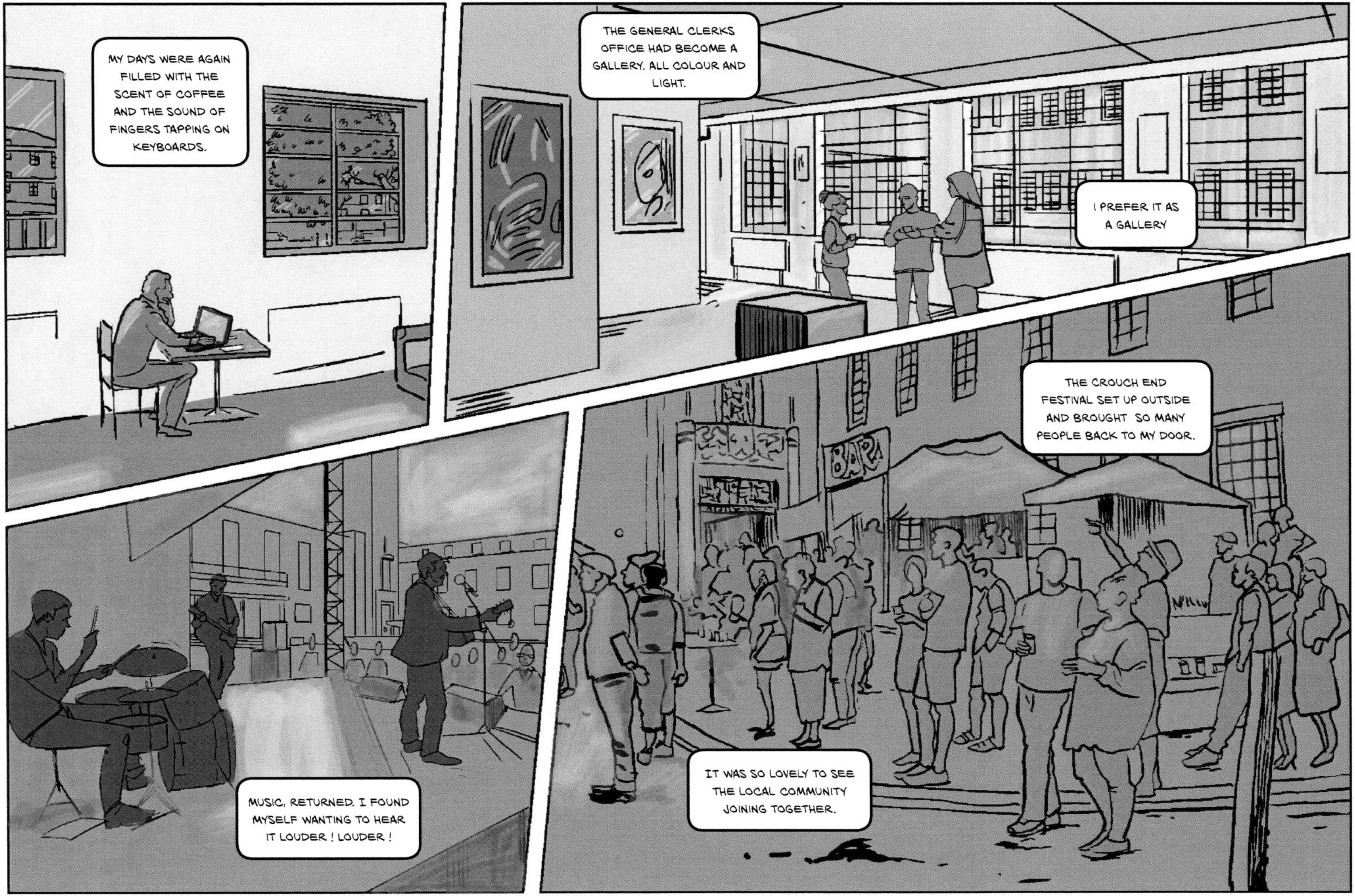
MY DAYS WERE AGAIN FILLED WITH THE SCENT OF COFFEE AND THE SOUND OF FINGERS TAPPING ON KEYBOARDS.
THE GENERAL CLERKS OFFICE HAD BECOME A GALLERY. ALL COLOUR AND LIGHT.
I PREFER IT AS A GALLERY
THE CROUCH END FESTIVAL SET UP OUTSIDE AND BROUGHT SO MANY PEOPLE BACK TO MY DOOR.
MUSIC, RETURNED. I FOUND MYSELF WANTING TO HEAR IT LOUDER ! LOUDER !
IT WAS SO LOVELY TO SEE THE LOCAL COMMUNITY JOINING TOGETHER.

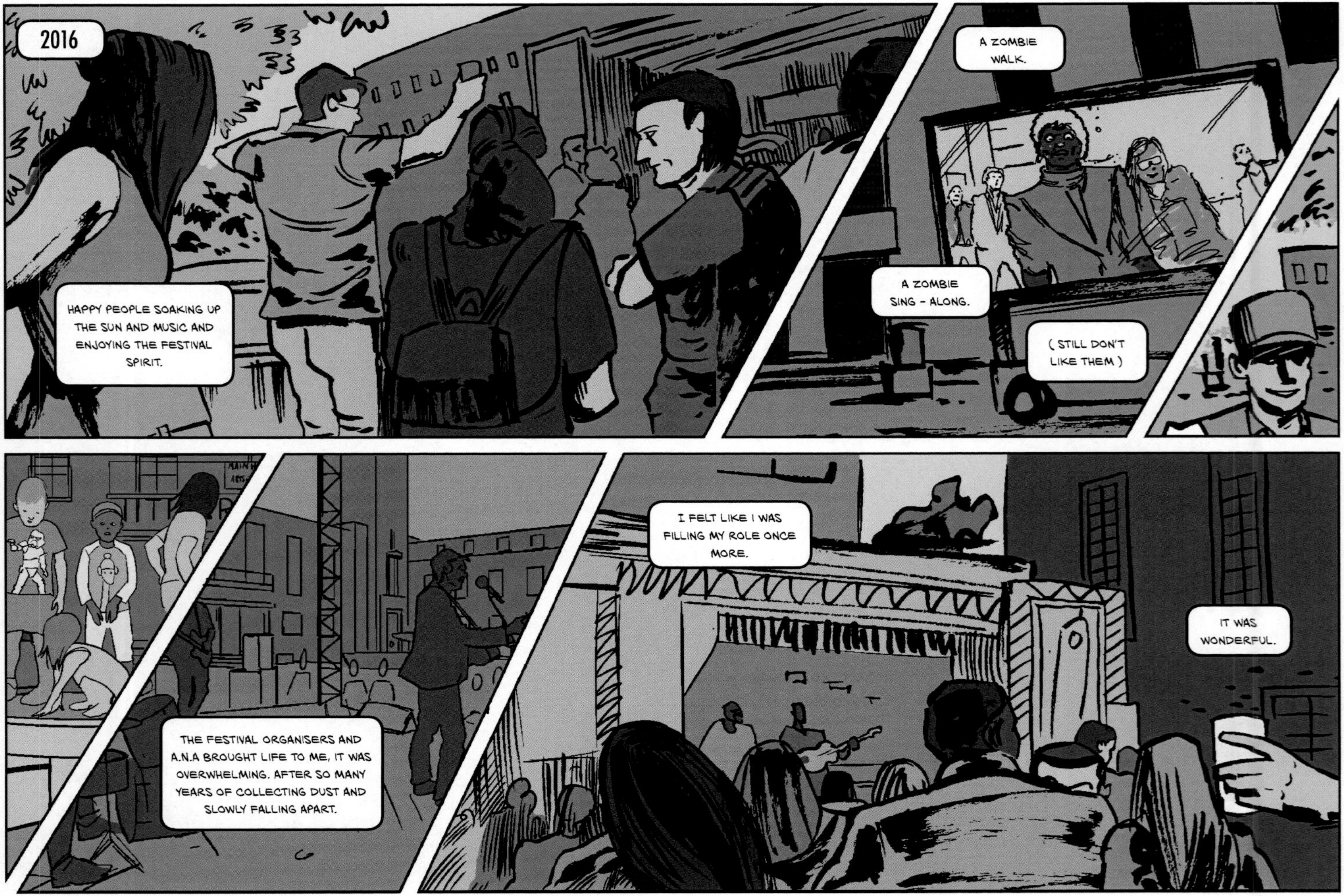
2016
HAPPY PEOPLE SOAKING UP THE SUN AND MUSIC AND ENJOYING THE FESTIVAL SPIRIT.
A ZOMBIE WALK.
A ZOMBIE SING - ALONG.
(STILL DON'T LIKE THEM)
THE FESTIVAL ORGANISERS AND A.N.A BROUGHT LIFE TO ME, IT WAS OVERWHELMING. AFTER SO MANY YEARS OF COLLECTING DUST AND SLOWLY FALLING APART.
I FELT LIKE I WAS FILLING MY ROLE ONCE MORE.
IT WAS WONDERFUL.

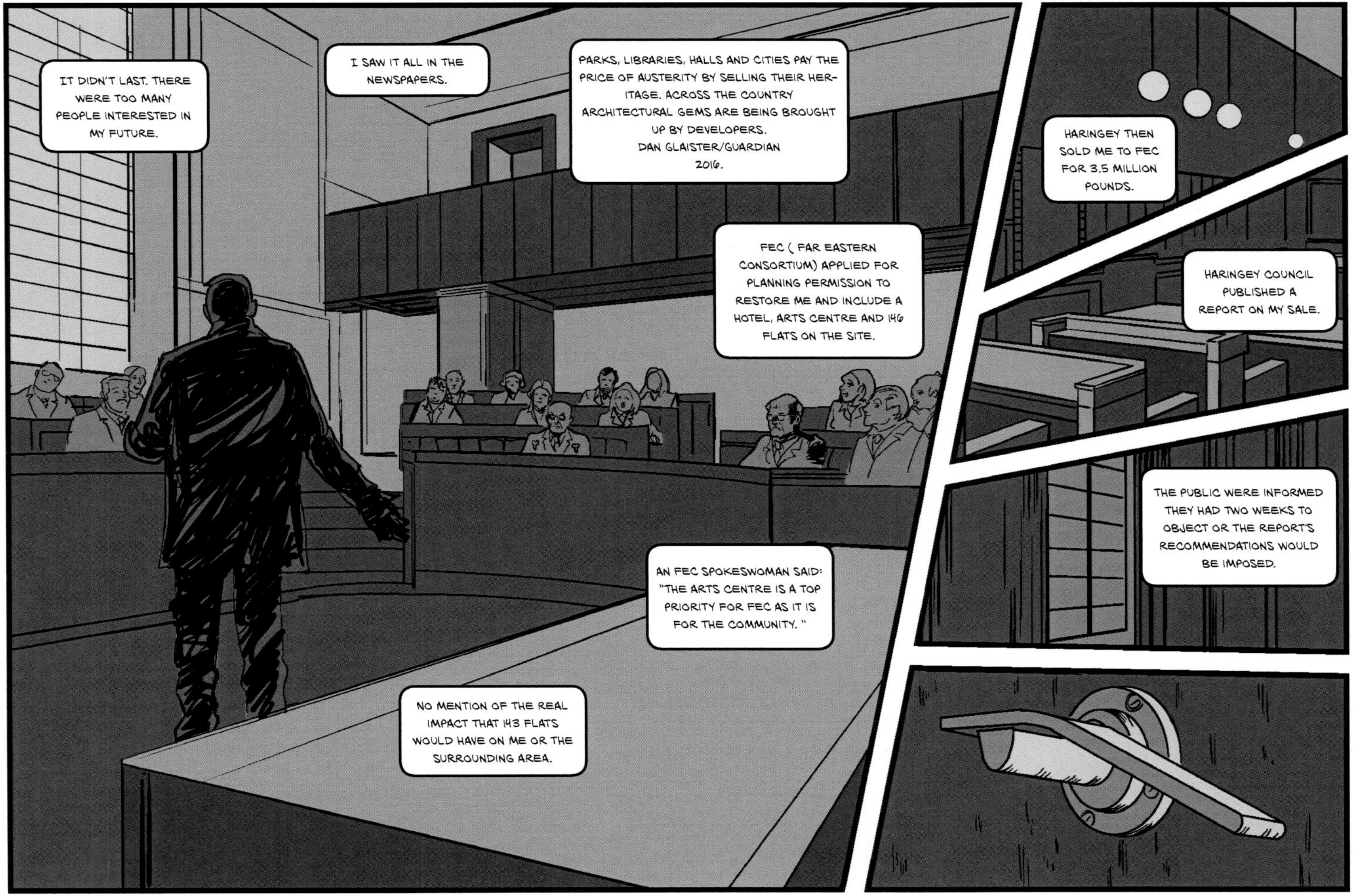
IT DIDN'T LAST. THERE WERE TOO MANY PEOPLE INTERESTED IN MY FUTURE.
I SAW IT ALL IN THE NEWSPAPERS.
PARKS, LIBRARIES, HALLS AND CITIES PAY THE PRICE OF AUSTERITY BY SELLING THEIR HER-ITAGE. ACROSS THE COUNTRY ARCHITECTURAL GEMS ARE BEING BROUGHT UP BY DEVELOPERS. DAN GLAISTER/GUARDIAN 2016.
FEC (FAR EASTERN CONSORTIUM) APPLIED FOR PLANNING PERMISSION TO RESTORE ME AND INCLUDE A HOTEL, ARTS CENTRE AND 146 FLATS ON THE SITE.
AN FEC SPOKESWOMAN SAID: "THE ARTS CENTRE IS A TOP PRIORITY FOR FEC AS IT IS FOR THE COMMUNITY. "
NO MENTION OF THE REAL IMPACT THAT 143 FLATS WOULD HAVE ON ME OR THE SURROUNDING AREA.
HARINGEY THEN SOLD ME TO FEC FOR 3.5 MILLION POUNDS.
HARINGEY COUNCIL PUBLISHED A REPORT ON MY SALE.
THE PUBLIC WERE INFORMED THEY HAD TWO WEEKS TO OBJECT OR THE REPORT'S RECOMMENDATIONS WOULD BE IMPOSED.

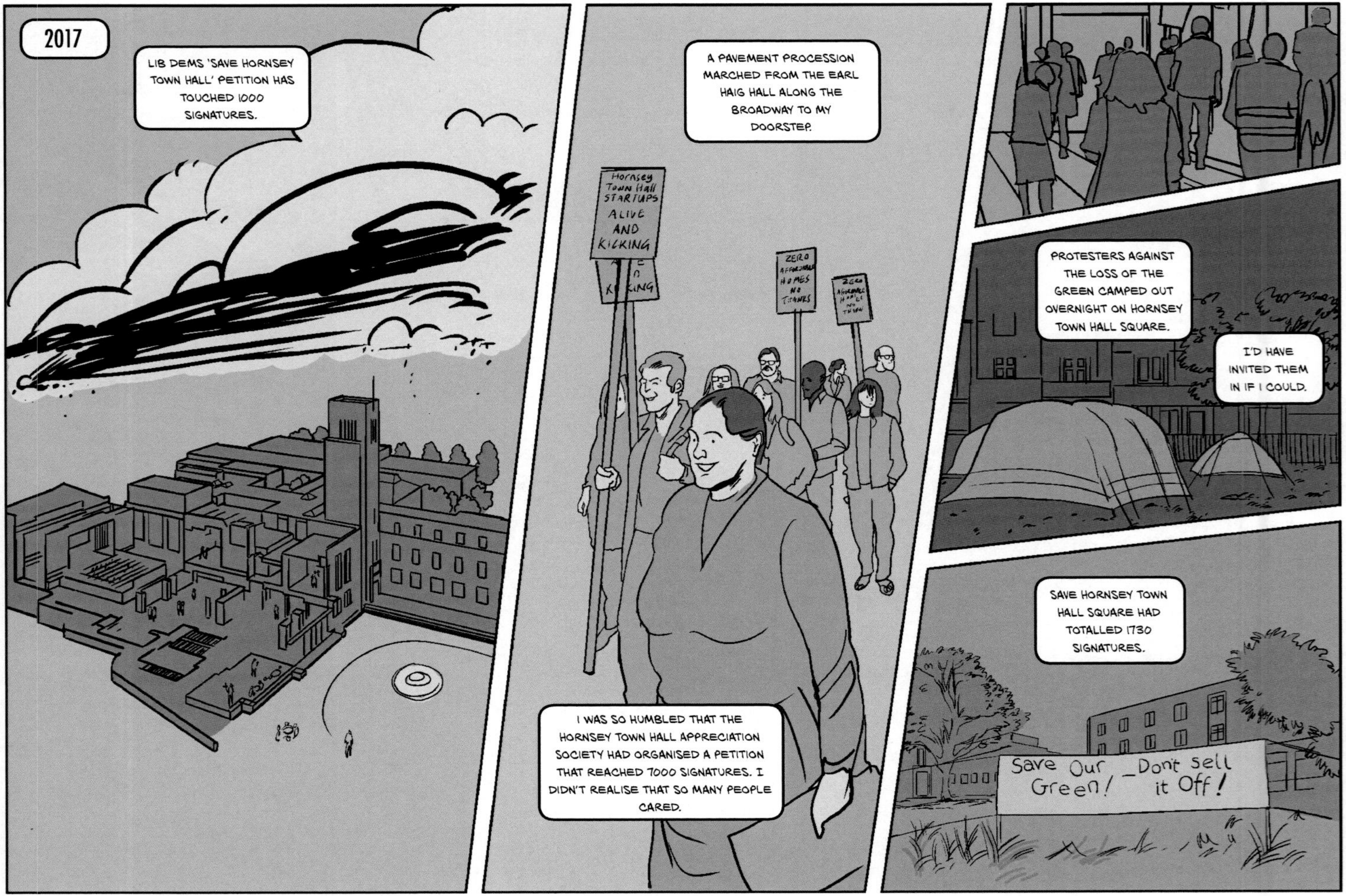
2017
LIB DEMS 'SAVE HORNSEY TOWN HALL' PETITION HAS TOUCHED 1000 SIGNATURES.
A PAVEMENT PROCESSION MARCHED FROM THE EARL HAIG HALL ALONG THE BROADWAY TO MY DOORSTEP.
Hornsey Town Hall STARTUPS ALIVE AND KICKING
ZERO AFFORDABLE HOMES NO THANKS
I WAS SO HUMBLED THAT THE HORNSEY TOWN HALL APPRECIATION SOCIETY HAD ORGANISED A PETITION THAT REACHED 7000 SIGNATURES. I DIDN'T REALISE THAT SO MANY PEOPLE CARED.
PROTESTERS AGAINST THE LOSS OF THE GREEN CAMPED OUT OVERNIGHT ON HORNSEY TOWN HALL SQUARE.
I'D HAVE INVITED THEM IN IF I COULD.
SAVE HORNSEY TOWN HALL SQUARE HAD TOTALLED 1730 SIGNATURES.
Save Our Green! _Don't sell it Off!

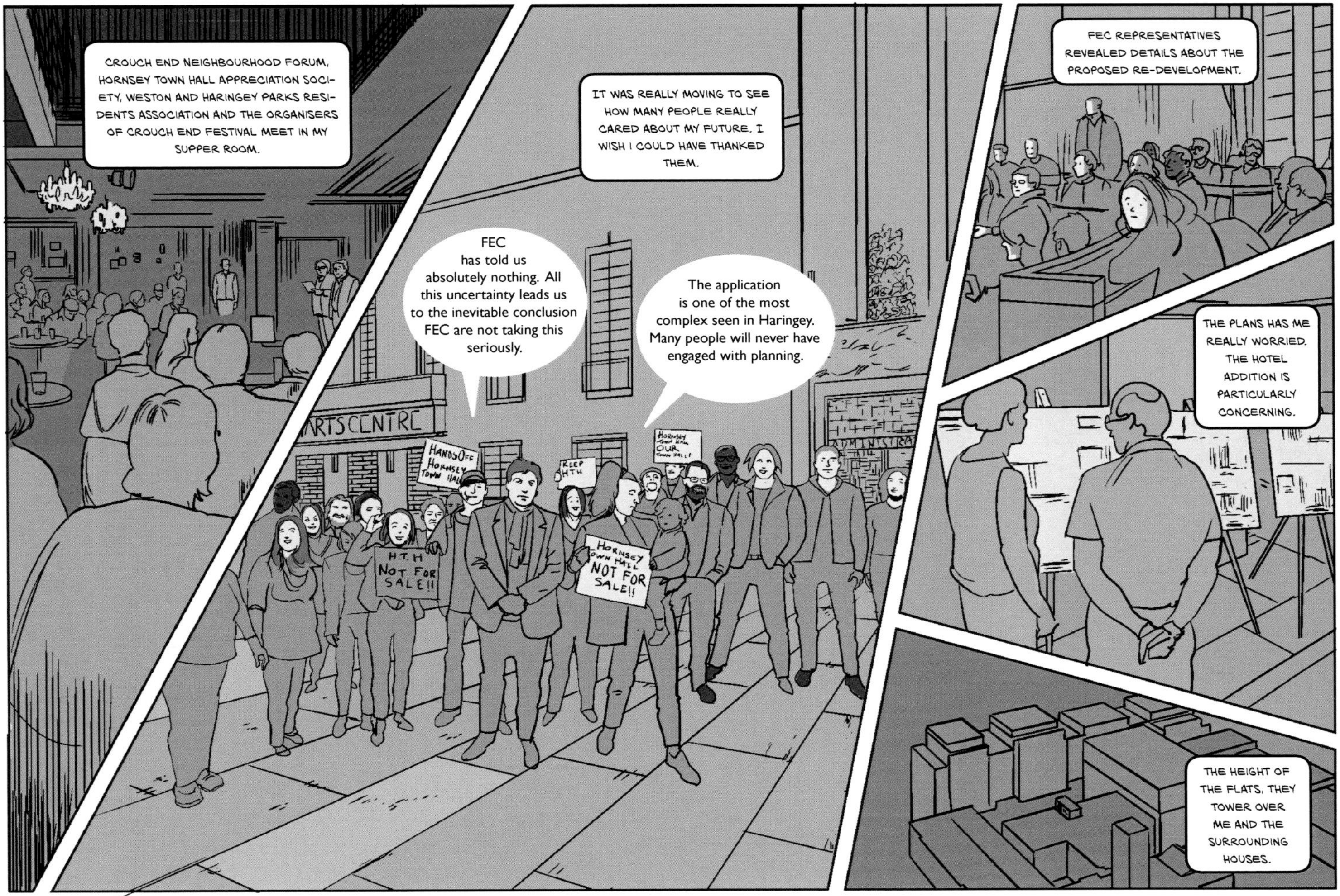
CROUCH END NEIGHBOURHOOD FORUM, HORNSEY TOWN HALL APPRECIATION SOCIETY, WESTON AND HARINGEY PARKS RESIDENTS ASSOCIATION AND THE ORGANISERS OF CROUCH END FESTIVAL MEET IN MY SUPPER ROOM.
IT WAS REALLY MOVING TO SEE HOW MANY PEOPLE REALLY CARED ABOUT MY FUTURE. I WISH I COULD HAVE THANKED THEM.
FEC has told us absolutely nothing. All this uncertainty leads us to the inevitable conclusion FEC are not taking this seriously.
The application is one of the most complex seen in Haringey. Many people will never have engaged with planning.
ARTS CENTRE
HANDS OFF HORNSEY TOWN HALL
KEEP HTH
H.T.H NOT FOR SALE!!
HORNSEY TOWN HALL NOT FOR SALE!!
FEC REPRESENTATIVES REVEALED DETAILS ABOUT THE PROPOSED RE-DEVELOPMENT.
THE PLANS HAS ME REALLY WORRIED. THE HOTEL ADDITION IS PARTICULARLY CONCERNING.
THE HEIGHT OF THE FLATS, THEY TOWER OVER ME AND THE SURROUNDING HOUSES.

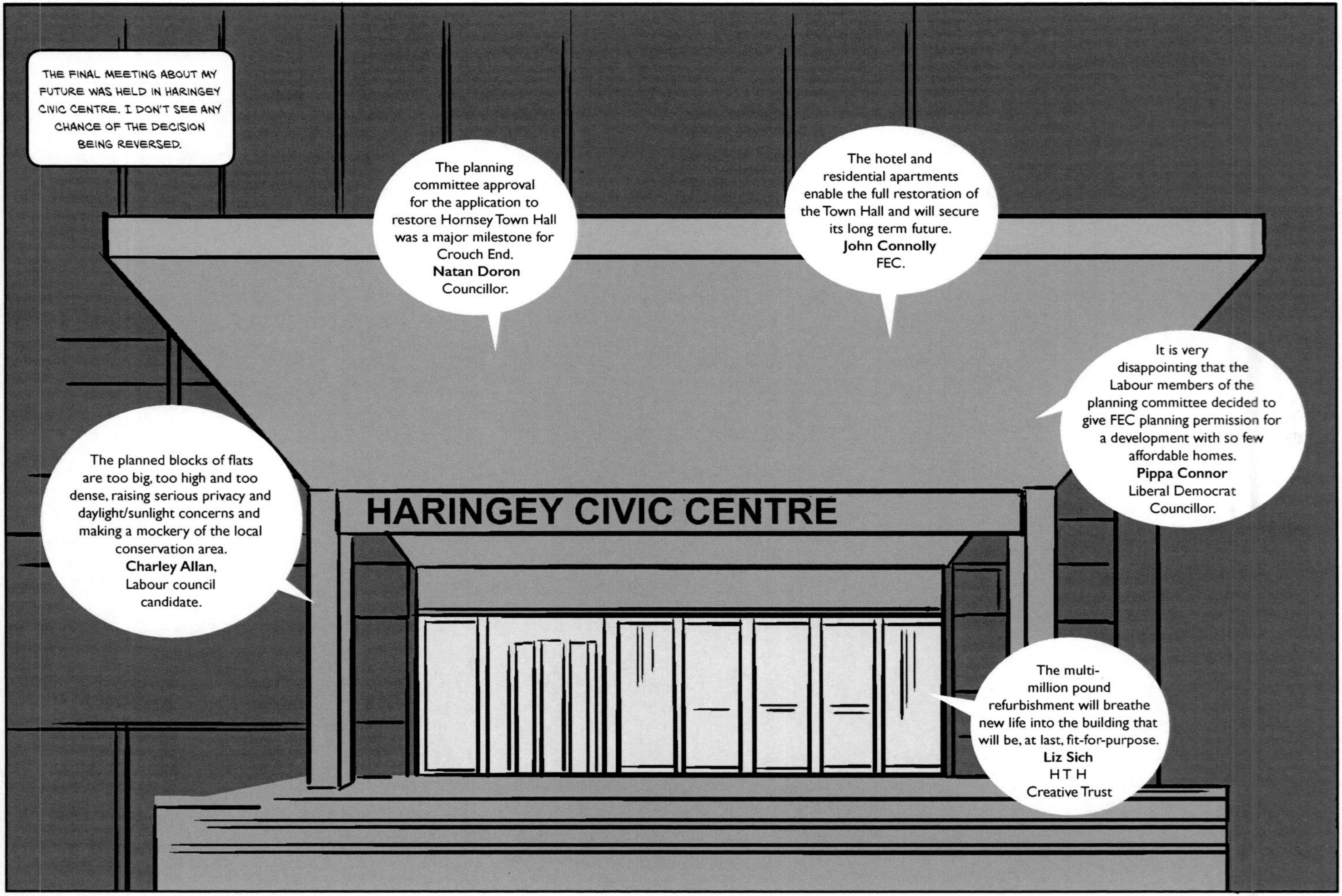
THE FINAL MEETING ABOUT MY FUTURE WAS HELD IN HARINGEY CIVIC CENTRE. I DON'T SEE ANY CHANCE OF THE DECISION BEING REVERSED.
The planning committee approval for the application to restore Hornsey Town Hall was a major milestone for Crouch End. **Natan Doron** Councillor.
The hotel and residential apartments enable the full restoration of the Town Hall and will secure its long term future. **John Connolly** FEC.
It is very disappointing that the Labour members of the planning committee decided to give FEC planning permission for a development with so few affordable homes. **Pippa Connor** Liberal Democrat Councillor.
The planned blocks of flats are too big, too high and too dense, raising serious privacy and daylight/sunlight concerns and making a mockery of the local conservation area. **Charley Allan**, Labour council candidate.
HARINGEY CIVIC CENTRE
The multi-million pound refurbishment will breathe new life into the building that will be, at last, fit-for-purpose. **Liz Sich** H T H Creative Trust

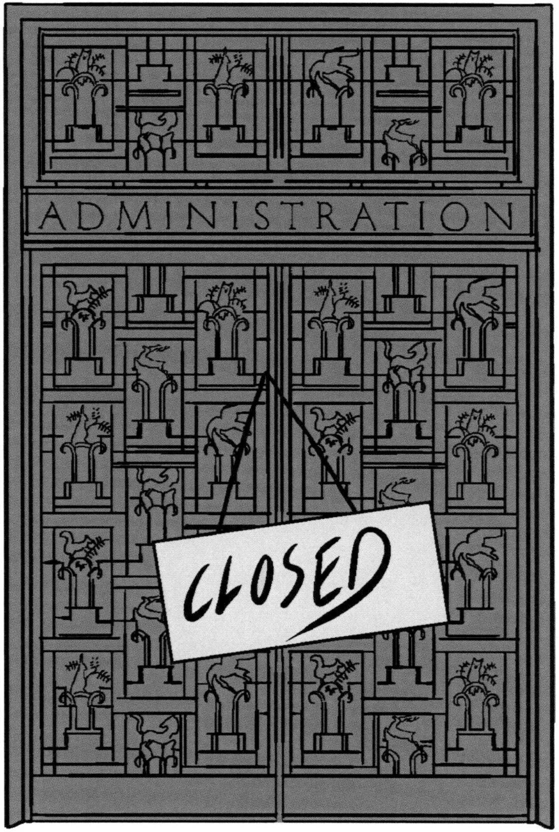
ADMINISTRATION
CLOSED

I WILL BE CLOSED SUMMER 2018. WHEN I'M REOPENED IN 2020 I WILL NO LONGER BE THE BUILDING DESIGNED BY MY DAD.

82 YEARS.

THAT'S NOT BAD, IS IT ?

Building are vital organisms they contain people who are doing something and it is people who matter not the buildings. Buildings should be designed as environments to make the lives of people more enjoyable against pleasant backgrounds. All to often buildings are not studied enough before they are designed. Economic influence, the elements of fashion and gimmick and the haste of developers who want the design almost overnight too often do not give the present day architecture time to create.
Architecture should be above transient fashion for after all buildings have to stand the test of time.

Reginald Uren
Architect
1965

THE
VOICE
OF THE
HALL

Credits and bibliography

A view from the community.

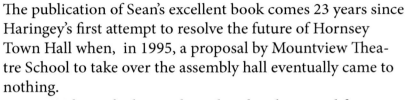

The publication of Sean's excellent book comes 23 years since Haringey's first attempt to resolve the future of Hornsey Town Hall when, in 1995, a proposal by Mountview Theatre School to take over the assembly hall eventually came to nothing.

Five years later, the borough, with a shrinking workforce, decided that it had no need for the building at all. When the decision dribbled out, several groups emerged to advise and cajole Haringey on what to do with this wonderful Grade II* building.

When asked, Haringey residents consistently said wanted the building to be kept in some sort of public (municipal or charitable) ownership and develop a new role by offering performance, education and community activities.

After years of neglect and only basic maintenance, HTH was

on the Heritage England at risk. Leaky roofs and subsidence were causing damage and there were rumours of asbestos restoration would cost at least £10m.

A cunning scheme was hatched to sell the land at the rear for housing to pay for the restoration with the balance coming from Heritage Lottery. A charitable arts trust would be given a long lease when they produced a workable restoration plan and water-tight business plan.

In 2010 the world financial crash came. Liquidity dried up, the housing market faltered. In addition, the UK won the Olympics and so for several years heritage lottery money was impossible to get. The scheme was doomed.

Enter Mountview (again) with a plan to come back to Crouch End and expand their student roll to 600 students. Unfortunately the figures didn't work. Instead they are on the verge of leaving

Haringey altogether for new premises in Southwark.

So, in 2104 Haringey, under a new CEO, decided they had had enough and resolved to get HTH off the Haringey books via a European disposal process.

I was part of the HTH Appreciation Society who tried to start a dialogue with ward councillors to revive the 2010 scheme; the car park had more than doubled in value and lottery money was flowing again. Obsessed with a "market led solution" and despite a 7 000 signature petition, Haringey refuse to talk.

Meanwhile, to keep the building warm, ANA were tossed the keys and grabbed the opportunity to show just what it could offer. After only three years and minimal investment (but a lot of hard work) ANA continue to work with the community to put on a dazzling programme of arts and performance and community events, offer spaces for classes and rent old offices to 90 small business giving employment to 130 local people.

The winning bidders, FEC, plan to build 146 flats, a luxury hotel, restaurants, bars and are required to restore HTH: they have appointed an operator for the residual a parts of the building.

It remains unclear what the operator will offer but, without access to public funding, many feel that it will be an arts centre in name rather than spirit.

The restoration is welcome but only time will tell whether the true potential of this wonderful, glorious building to serve the community is at last released.

David Winskill

March 2018

I am a London-based cartoonist who has attended a variety of comics related events, both locally and internationally. I have also been involved with collectives and was a founding member of London Underground Comics, and currently involved with The Crouch End Festival. I have also organised and curated **CECAF,** Crouch Ends first cartoon festival. I've produced numerous mini comics and books for my Phatcomics imprint, including acclaimed titles such as Ed, Twelve Hour Shift and Dark Matters. Away from self published titles I'm working on Vol 3 of Necessary Monsters (First comics) and was awarded an Arts Council grant for the arts. This enabled me to work on my first graphic novel, which you have just read and was published by **Soaring Penguin press.**
I am currentley working on a new project with Douglas Noble, titled **Black leather.**

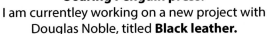

Comics are the best !

Thank you to the following people for their time and help.
Completing this project would not have been possible without input from the following greats.
John Anderson and Soaring Penguin.
Art Consultants Glen Martson and Paul Dewis.
Steve Amor, Dave Winskill, for the coffee and insider knowledge.
The Crouch End Festival, Amanda C, Chris C, Chris A, Bev C.
A.N.A - Nick, Asa and Alex. Hornsey Town Hall Arts Center, John and Dani.
Bruce Castle musem - Clare And Deborah.
Crouch End Historical Society.
Ladies do Comics, Rachael and Wallis.
Cass Arts and Mim.
Nicola Streeten.
Gareth Brookes, Nick Abadzis, Francesca Cassavetti, Daniel Merlin Goodbrey.
The Malta crew.
TCAF.
Andy Oliver.
The Earl Haig, The Queens.
A very sepcial thanks to Douglas Noble.
Special thanks to The Arts Council of England for the support and input.
Finally my flatmate, who has to endure the whole colourfield of emotions i've displayed through this project.

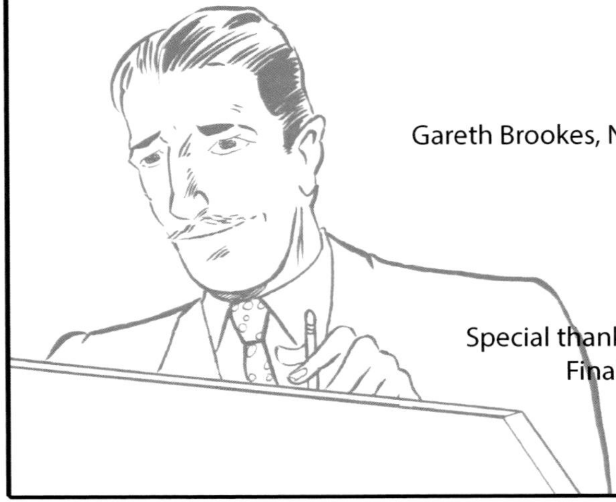

Publications

The Hornsey Journal	
The Hornsey Journal Supplement	
Civic Pride In Hornsey	Bridget Cherry
Town Halls	A. Calvely Cotton.
The Architecture of England	Doreen Yarwood.
Modern Architecture	Kenneth Frampton.

Organisations

RIBA (Royal Institute Of British Architects).
The V and A.
Hornsey Historical Society.
Bruce Castle Museum.
Crouch End Festival.
ANA.
Hornsey Town Hall Arts Centre.

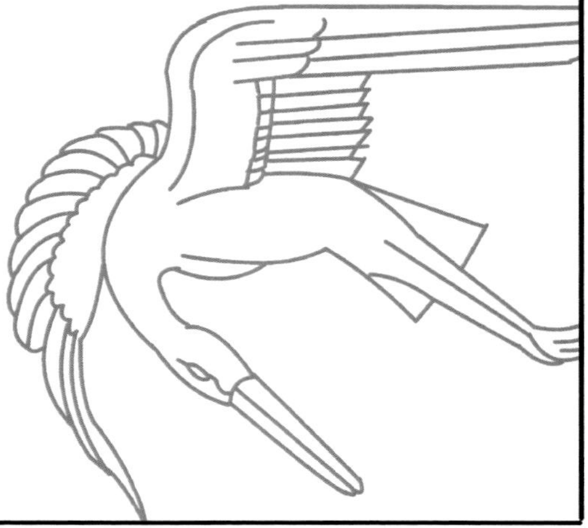

LOTTERY FUNDED

ARTS COUNCIL ENGLAND

Supported using public funding by

ARTS COUNCIL ENGLAND

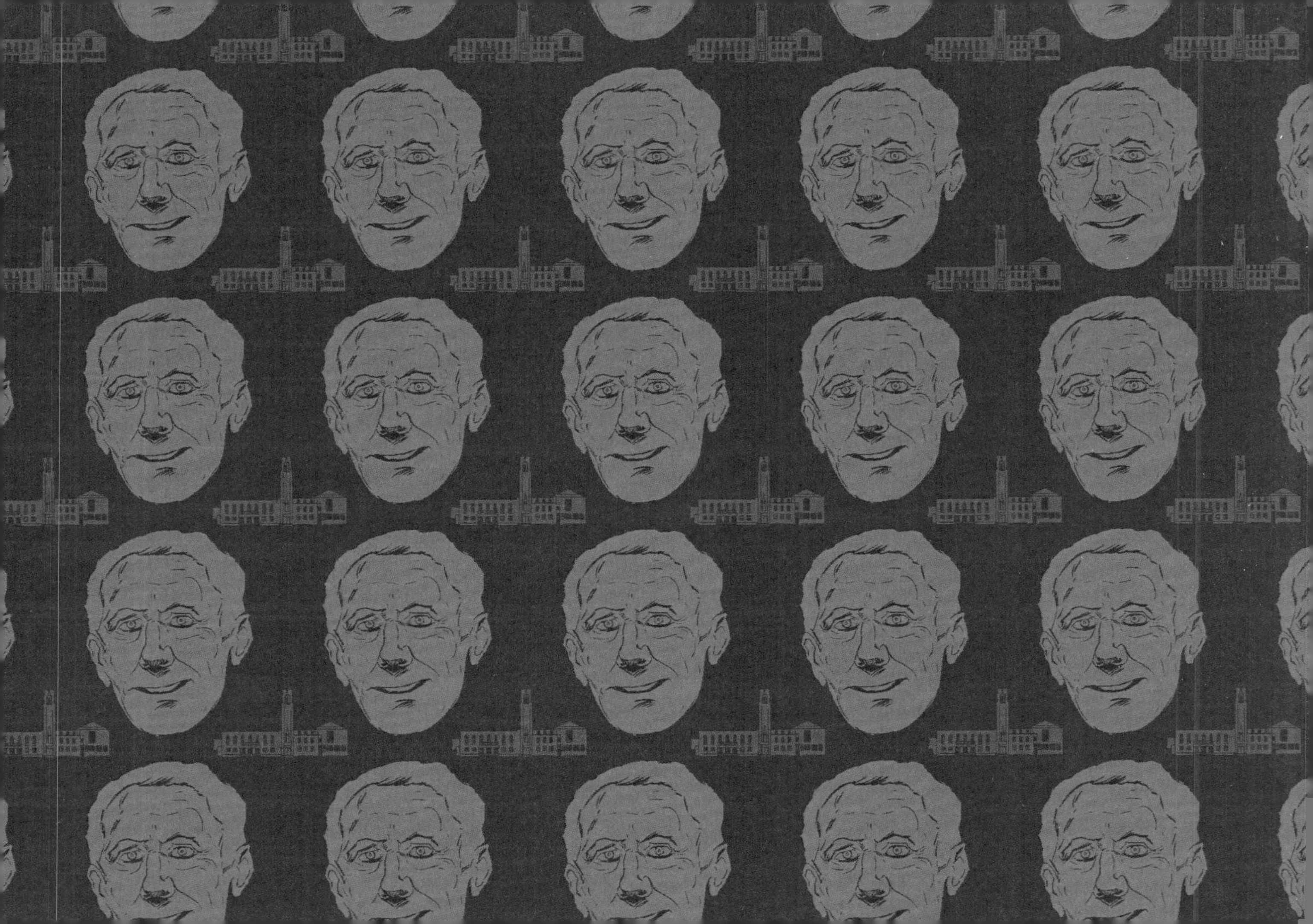